Little Jack Horner

A pantomime

Paul Reakes

Samuel French – London
New York – Sydney – Toronto – Hollywood

CHARACTERS

Bertie
Gertie } two pupils
Patience, a teacher
Dame Dimwit, the headmistress
Little Jack Horner
King Marmaduke, a ruler
The Queen, "his" ruler
Prince Peter, their son
Graball, the evil Lord Chamberlain
Rosa, a gypsy girl
Meg, an old gypsy woman
Vasaleno, the gypsy chief
Bopo, his side-kick
Pedro, the pony
Chorus of Schoolchildren, Townsfolk, King's men, Guards, Heralds, Guests, Gypsies

SYNOPSIS OF SCENES

ACT I

Scene 1 The playground of Dame Dimwit's school
Scene 2 A street
Scene 3 The Royal Palace
Scene 4 The street again
Scene 5 A classroom in the school

ACT II

Scene 1 The gypsy camp in the woods
Scene 2 A pathway in the woods
Scene 3 The classroom
Scene 4 The pathway in the woods
Scene 5 The haunted ruins at midnight
Scene 6 The last lesson
Scene 7 The Grand Finale

MUSIC PLOT

ACT I

1.	Song and dance	Chorus and Children
2.	Song	Patience, Bertie, Gertie and Children
3.	Comedy song	Dame Dimwit
4.	Song and dance	Jack and Dancers
5.	Duet	Peter and Patience
6.	Comedy duet and dance	King and Girl
7.	Song and dance	Peter, Chorus and Dancers
8.	Comedy song	Dame, King, Peter, Patience
9.	Duet and dance	Jack and Rose
10.	Song and dance	Bertie, Gertie and Children

ACT II

11.	Song and dance	Chorus and Dancers
12.	Song and dance	Rosa, Bopo, Chorus and Dancers
13.	Song	Jack, Rosa and Chorus
14.	Song	Patience, Bertie, Gertie and Children
15.	Song	Peter, Patience, Children and Chorus
16.	Song and dance	Chorus and Dancers
17.	Song	All
18.	Sing-a-long	Dame, Bertie, Gertie and Audience
19.	Grand finale	All

A licence issued by Samuel French Ltd to perform this play does NOT include permission to use any copyright music in the performance. The notice printed below on behalf of the Performing Right Society should be carefully read.

PRODUCTION NOTES

Staging

The pantomime offers opportunities for elaborate staging, but can be produced quite simply if facilities and funds are limited. There are five sets:

> The playground of Dame Dimwit's school
> The Royal Palace (this can be used for Finale)
> A classroom in the school
> The gypsy camp in the woods
> The haunted ruins at midnight

These scenes are interlinked with tabs or frontcloth scenes.

The **oven** is backless and fixed to a side wing with a corresponding opening. This enables the pies to be passed through to the children, unseen by the audience. "Crazy foam" is sprayed over the King and Dame as the oven explodes with bangs, flashes and smoke. The **Cookery Lesson** scene must be a well-rehearsed "slap-stick" routine for the Dame and Bertie and Gertie. The choice of comic business is left to the individual director. Plenty of fun with flour, water and rolling pins, etc. A protective stage cloth is advisable for this scene. The **Tall Ghost** is simply Gertie sitting on Bertie's shoulders and both covered in a long white "ghost" sheet with eyeholes for visibility. Plenty of rehearsals are advisable. However, if this is considered too dangerous or impractical, they can appear as individual ghosts. After the gypsies are scared off, they can bump into each other, fall over and ruin the "ghoulish" effect.

Characters and costumes

Bertie and **Gertie** are a cheeky, mischievous pair of schoolkids. These parts should be played by adults for the best comedy effect. Ideally Bertie should be tall and lanky, and Gertie short and dumpy. They are involved in plenty of slap-stick and audience participation. **Bertie** is scruffy, dressed in a tiny school cap, a too small blazer and short trousers—an outsized "Just William"! **Gertie** has comic pigtails, a straw boater and a short, baggy gym-slip, and perhaps a couple of front teeth missing—a refugee from St Trinian's! In Act II they get to wear comic boy scout and girl guide outfits.

Patience is a pretty young teacher. She has a sweet singing voice and a charming manner but is never soppy or simpering. All her scholastic costumes are plain but attractive. A delightful dress is worn for the Palace scene in Act I. Finale costume.

Dame Dimwit is the Headmistress. A comical old girl who likes to be thought "quite posh", but is really as common as muck! She sports a pair of pince-nez, a variety of comic mortarboards and is never without her trusty cane. In addition to her crazy scholastic attire, she wears an outrageous costume for the Palace scene in Act I and a ludicrous "nature ramble" outfit in Act II. Special finale costume.

Little Jack Horner is a pleasant, likeable young chap. Preferably a female part of the "Aladdin" type, but could be played by a teenage male. The part calls for some sincere acting, a good singing voice and dancing ability. One costume will suffice. Special finale costume.

King Marmaduke is a short, comical old buffoon. In spite of being completely dominated by the Queen, he is fun loving and still has an eye for the ladies—even Dame Dimwit! He is involved in plenty of audience participation. Comic regal costumes with a crown that refuses to stay in place. Finale costume.

The Queen is a large, haughty "battleaxe". She has a very domineering voice and manner, and the part should be played with complete austerity— making her sudden lapse into frivolity at the end even more surprising and funny. Grand regal costumes. Finale costume.

Prince Peter (principal boy) is a handsome young gentleman who is in no way a snob. He is romantic, has a keen sense of royal duty and a gorgeous pair of legs. His costumes should be striking without being "foppish". Finale costume.

Graball is the wicked Lord Chamberlain. He is an out-and-out villain. With the royals he is grovelling and servile, but shows his true nasty nature when dealing with the others and the audience. Just in case there is any doubt about his villainy, he is garbed completely in black.

Rosa is a dark young gypsy beauty. She is tough, spirited and can take care of herself. Her only sign of weakness is shown in her concern for Jack for whom she has fallen in a big way. The part calls for some strong acting and a good singing voice. Colourful, picturesque gypsy costumes. Finale costume.

Meg is a kindly old gypsy woman—or so it first appears. She is the holder of a dark secret that causes a sensation. Colourful gypsy costume.

Vasaleno is the villainous gypsy chief. A fat, swarthy individual with an eye-patch and a greasy moustache to twirl. He is boastful and overbearing but a complete coward when up against Rosa or Pedro the pony. Exaggerated gypsy costume. He gets to wear a black cloak and black mask. He only appears in Act II.

Bopo is his dopey, lovable little side-kick. As Vasaleno uses him for a punch bag, he should get lots of sympathy from the audience. Comic gypsy costume with huge earrings. He also gets to wear a black cloak and mask. He only appears in Act II.

Pedro the pony is a cute little four-legged friend. However, at the sight of Vasaleno or the mention of his name, he becomes an untamed bronco. A good pony skin with movable eyelids and jaw. Only appears in Act II.

The **Children** appear as pupils of Dame Dimwit's school and young gypsies. They are involved in the action and musical numbers.

The **Dancers** are dream characters, kings men, luncheon guests and gypsies.

The **Chorus** appear as townsfolk, four guards, heralds, luncheon guests and gypsies. All participate in the action and musical numbers.

Lime Juice House

ACT I

Scene 1

The playground of Dame Dimwit's school

Prominent on stage L is the school. It has a practical archway surmounted with the legend "DIMWIT'S SKOOL". Across the back runs a low wall broken in the centre by the school gates. The side wings represent playground walls. The backcloth shows a quaint town square with the Royal Palace in the distance. The school and walls are daubed with comic graffiti, "TEECHER IS A TWIT!" "DOWN WITH SKOOL", etc.

Before the CURTAIN *rises the school bell is heard ringing. At rise, to the tune of "Boys and girls come out to play", the townsfolk are discovered bringing their children to school through the gates. Some are being dragged unwillingly, some are having their noses wiped and hair combed, others are being restrained from fighting. The music changes to the opening number and everyone breaks into song*

Song 1

During the song the children can have a dance routine incorporating playground games—leap-frog, hopscotch, etc.

After the song, a loud honking is heard off-stage. Gertie charges on through the gateway, pushing a pram. It is brightly painted and decorated with L-plates, stickers and aerials with flags, etc. A large, old-fashioned motor horn is fixed to one side. Bertie is sitting in the pram, waving an enormous lollipop and honking the horn

Gertie pushes the pram around the stage, much to the annoyance of the townsfolk and the delight of the children. After the pram has run over a few toes . . .

The townsfolk exit

Gertie brings the pram to a sudden halt

Gertie (*to Bertie*) Get out! It's my turn! My turn!
Bertie (*staying put*) NAA! Tough toe-nails! (*He pokes his tongue out at her*)
Gertie You rotten smelly! (*She grabs the pram and shakes it violently*) Get out! Get out! Get out!

She succeeds in tipping Bertie out of the pram and he lands with a thump on his rump. The children roar with laughter as he hops about holding his tender rear. Gertie starts to clamber into the pram, but Bertie grabs her gym-slip and pulls her down. She lands with a thump and sits there, wailing loudly. Bertie and the children hoot with laughter. In a fury, Gertie snatches the lollipop away from Bertie and pushes it down the front of his shorts. He makes a wry face and walks around bow-legged. Gertie and the children love his discomfort. After some contortions, he extracts the lollipop. He grabs one of Gertie's pigtails and pulls it hard. She screams and screams. Bertie bends double with laughter and Gertie kicks him in the pants. They fight. The children cheer them on loudly

> *Patience, a pretty young teacher, enters from the school. She sees the fight, moves down and claps her hands*

Patience Children! Children!

The children go silent but Bertie and Gertie continue to fight. Patience moves in and pulls them apart

> *During the following dialogue, a couple of children remove the pram off* R *then return*

Bertie! Gertie! Stop it! Shame on you. Fighting again!

Bertie 'Tain't my fault, miss! 'Twas Nora Batty over there!

Gertie 'E started it, miss! 'E pulled my 'air!

Bertie Didn't!

Gertie Did!

Bertie Didn't!

Gertie (*stamping her feet*) Did! Did! Did!

Bertie Oh, go and boil yer 'ead!!

They charge at each other but Patience holds them apart

Patience You ought to be ashamed of yourselves. Fighting on such a beautiful morning as this. Look, the sun is shining. The birds are singing. The bees are buzzing, and all the flowers and trees are bursting with happiness.

Bertie
Gertie } (*together to the audience, in utter disgust*) Yuck!

Patience (*to the children*) Oh, it's wonderful to be alive, isn't it children?

Children (*enthusiastic*) Yes, Miss Patience!

Bertie (*to them*) Creeps!

Patience It makes you feel like jumping for joy, doesn't it?

Children (*as before*) Yes, Miss Patience!

Gertie (*to one of the girls*) Naa! Teacher's pet! (*She pokes her tongue out at the girl*)

Patience I don't know about you, but there's only one thing I feel like doing on such a splendid morning as this.

Bertie (*to the audience*) Look out, folks! There's a song comin' up!

The music starts

> (*To the audience*) Wot did I tell ya!

He and Gertie groan loudly and start to creep away. Patience stops them and sings

Song 2

After the song, the school bell is heard ringing from inside the school

Patience Here comes Dame Dimwit! (*She claps her hands*) Children! Get into line! Line up for your headmistress.

Bertie, Gertie and the children form a line with lots of pushing and shoving

> *Dame Dimwit appears in the school archway, ringing a large bell. She pauses for a moment, then enters, trips on her gown and falls over*

Bertie, Gertie and the children hoot with laughter. Patience claps her hands and "Shhs" them into silence. Dame Dimwit sits up with difficulty and Bertie lets out a snort of laughter

Dame Silence in class! If I hear one snig of a snigger, I'll give the whole school a hundred lines! (*She yelps with pain*) Ow!! What's that?! (*She pulls the bell out from under her*) Now I know what's meant by droppin' a clanger! (*Rubbing her rear and looking at the bell*) Oo! I think I've dented me donger! Well, don't just stand there, Miss Patience, 'elp me up!

Patience helps her to her feet. Dame gives Patience the bell then makes a great business of adjusting her mortarboard, pince-nez, gown, etc. Bertie and Gertie mimic her actions to the children. Dame sees this and creeps up behind them, rolling up the sleeves of her cane arm. The children see her and retreat, while Bertie and Gertie continue their comic capers. Eventually they sense something, turn and see the Dame. They pretend to be playing "pat-a-cake". Dame swishes her cane and they quickly retreat

(*To the children*) Good-morning, pupils.
Children (*sing-song*) Good-morning, Dame Dimwit.
Dame (*to the audience, coming forward*) Good-morning, pupils.

A few replies

Oh, come along! That will never do. Wake up at the back! I want a nice "Good-morning, Dame Dimwit". Good-morning pupils!

A few more replies

Dear, dear, dear! What's the matter with you all? You're half asleep!
Patience Excuse me, Dame Dimwit, (*indicating the audience*) these aren't your pupils.
Dame Ain't they? ... er ... I mean, isn't they? (*She adjusts her glasses and peers at the audience*) Oh, no! They isn't, is they! (*Aside to Patience*) They look like those horrible hooligans from (*local school*). Fancy making a silly mistake like that. I really must get my eyes examined.
Bertie Yeah! An' yer 'ead!
Dame (*spinning around*) *What* did you say?
Bertie I never said nufink, miss!
Dame (*appalled*) "I never said *nufink*"!!! What a way to speak! Where's your grammar?
Bertie At 'ome with me granfer!

He and the children laugh. Dame swishes her cane and they go silent

Dame Stupid boy! Take a hundred lines! "I must not pull my headmistress's leg!"

Bertie *Pull* it! I couldn't even *lift* it!

Dame raises her cane and Bertie runs back and hides behind Gertie

Dame Miss Patience, isn't it time the children were at their lessons?

Patience Yes, Dame Dimwit. Come along children.

She exits into the school and the children file in after her

Bertie and Gertie remain

Gertie (*hopping about and waving her hand*) Miss! Miss! Miss!

Dame You know where it is, dear!

Gertie No, miss! We've got sumfink to tell you, miss!

Dame What?

Bertie Some of the kids 'ave bin sayin' some nasty fings about you, miss!

Dame Oh, have they indeed! What sort of things?

Gertie They said you didn't 'ave the brains of a donkey, miss!

Dame (*exploding*) What!!!

Bertie But we stuck up for you, miss!

Dame (*patting them both on the head*) They're dears.

Gertie Yeah! We told 'em you did!

Dame How kind, I—(*Sudden dawning*) You!!!

Laughing, Bertie and Gertie beat a quick exit into the school

(*To the audience*) Don't let those juvenile detergents put you off. This is a very high-class school. It's approved. I'm the headmistress and you should see the size of my diplomas. Who tittered? I won't have titters in my class! (*To a child in audience*) Was it *you*? Yes, you! You with the funny hair cut (*or ad lib to suit*)! (*To an adult*) And that big boy, over there! Stop doing *that* or I'll make you stand in the corner! Oh, don't think you're too grown up. I've handled much bigger boys than you in my time! (*To all*) Some very famous people have attended this school. Des O'Connor learnt how to sing here and Gary Lineker used to dribble all over the playing fields. Maggie Thatcher was head girl here and Arthur Scargill was head boy. That was Scargill *minor*, of course. (*Very snooty*) I bet your school isn't as good as this one, is it?

"*Yes!*"

Oh, no it isn't!

"Oh yes it is!" routine

Right! Just for that I'm going to give you all a test! I'll sing a little song and I want to see how good you are at coming in with the chorus! (*To pianist or conductor*) Ready Mr/Mrs Lloyd Webber?

Song 3

After the song, Bertie and Gertie enter from the school

Gertie (*hopping about waving her hand*) Miss! Miss! Miss!

Dame You know where it is!

Gertie No, miss! (*With evil relish*) Little Jack Horner's late again, miss!

Dame What!!!

Bertie You said, the next time 'e was late you'd give 'im six of the best! Cor! (*He rubs his hands*)

Dame Oh, lacerate me Latin and fracture me French! That boy's the limit! (*To the audience*) Every morning he's late for school! And the excuses! Yesterday he was late because his mother was helping out James Bond! And the day before his father was (*topical gag*)! I've given him lines until I'm blue in the face! Today, he gets *this*! (*She swishes her cane*)

Bertie Yeah! Give 'im a *branch* line!

Dame I've had enough! It's got to stop! I've been very soft up till now!

Gertie You can say that again!

Dame I must have strict discipline in my school. I shall follow in my father's footsteps!

Bertie (*to the audience*) Straight down to the (*local pub*)!

Dame He was a great believer in discipline. He was an army man! A general!

Gertie (*to the audience*) General accident!

She and Bertie giggle together. Dame Dimwit moves behind them, rolling up her cane arm

Dame I also had an uncle in the army. He was a major.

Bertie }
Gertie } (*together*) A major?

Dame Major-Bum Sore!!

She swishes her cane and chases Bertie and Gertie into school

A slight pause, then Little Jack Horner enters at the back and creeps in through the gates. He looks cautiously at the school then comes forward

Jack (*to the audience, waving*) Hallo everybody! Hi kids! I'm Little Jack Horner. Well, here I am, late for school again! Has old Dimwit noticed?

"*Yes!*"

Oh, never mind! I've got a real good excuse ready to fool the old twerp!

Unseen by him, Bertie and Gertie peep out from the school archway. They see Jack, cackle fiendishly and disappear again

(*To the audience*) Are you ever late for school, kids? (*By play with children in the audience*) Well, *I'm* late *every* morning! Waking up and getting out of bed has something to do with it, I think. I have some really smashing dreams, you know. In my dreams I meet all the fantastic people you'd never meet in real life.

Song 4

Jack sings, then the lighting changes to "dream" dance sequence. A little ground mist will help

Various characters from the fantasy worlds of film, TV and comic book enter the scene and dance with Jack. After the dance they exit

The stage grows dark and Jack is left alone to finish the song in a single spotlight

Dame (*off, after the applause*) Jack Horner!!!

The Lights snap back to normal and we return to reality!

Dame Dimwit enters from the school followed by Patience, Bertie, Gertie and the children

(*Grabbing Jack by the ear*) Jack Horner! You bad boy! Late again! You should have been here at nine o'clock!

Jack Why, what happened?

Dame Don't be flippin' flippant with me, young man! You've had enough warnings. Now it's whacko time! (*She swishes her cane*) Bend over, I'm going to give yer whatnot a polish!

Bertie and Gertie cackle with devilish glee

Jack Wait, miss! I couldn't help being late! Honest! Let me explain——

Dame Oh, no! I'm not listening to any more of your fibs! Bend over! You'll be a real *deadend* kid, when I've finished with you!

Jack (*desperate*) Miss!!

Dame Miss?! Oh, don't worry, I shan't miss! Over!!

Jack bends over. Bertie and Gertie are watching with evil relish. Dame Dimwit limbers up and is about to take a swing at Jack, when ...

The townsfolk rush on in a very excited state

Man Dame Dimwit! Dame Dimwit! Stop! You can't do that now!

Dame *Can't* I?! You just watch me! (*She lifts her cane*)

Woman The King and Queen are coming!

Dame What?!

Man They'll be here any minute!

Dame (*flustered*) Oh! The King and Queen ... oh! ... comin' 'ere ... I ... I must go an' titivate meself! Gangway!!

She rushes into the school, followed by Bertie and Gertie

Jack escapes off R

The townsfolk and children move to the sides

A Herald enters through the gates. Fanfare

Herald Make way! Make way for their Royal Majesties, the King and Queen of Pantomania and their son, his Royal Highness, Prince Peter!

Fanfare. To suitable music, the King and Queen enter. She is a large, domineering battleaxe, he is a short, round lovable old nitwit. They are followed by handsome Prince Peter and the sinister Lord Graball who carries a golden casket. Four guards bring up the rear

The crowd wave and cheer. The Queen walks about giving the royal wave. Peter stops by Patience and is soon in quiet conversation with her. The King spots a pretty girl in the crowd and flirts with her. She gives him a curtsy and he returns it with a low bow. His crown slips down over his eyes

King (*in a panic*) Ah! Help! I can't see! Everything's gone black! Ooh!! (*He blunders down to the Queen*) Who put the lights out?! (*He pulls his crown up*) Phew! That's better! (*He sees the Queen glaring at him and reacts*) Ugh! No, it isn't!

Queen Marmaduke!

King Yes, dear?

Queen (*indicating the audience*) The *riff-raff* are gathered before us. Greet them.

King (*waving to the audience*) Watch'er me old cock sparrows!

Queen (*slapping him*) Not like that! Oh! let *me* do it! (*To the audience*) Greetings to *all*—(*she gestures grandly and knocks the King over*)—our loyal subjects' My husband and I . . . (*She looks for the King*) Where is he now?! (*She sees the King on the ground*) What are you doing down there?!

King (*doing so*) Gettin' up, dear!

Queen (*to the audience*) Loyal subjects, we are here today to . . . (*to the King*) . . . you should be doing this! You are the King after all!

King Nice of you to remember, dear. (*To the audience*) Soyal lubjects! . . . er . . . loyal objects! (*He mimics the Queen's voice*) We are here today to . . . er . . . to . . . er . . . (*To the Queen*) Why *are* we 'ere, dear?

Queen Oh, you're hopeless! Let *me* do the talking!

King (*to the audience*) That'll make a nice change!

Queen (*to the audience*) Subjects, we are here today to allow you to feast your unworthy eyes on a royal treasure.

King Oh! Thank you, dear! (*He does a comic twirl and pose*)

Queen (*slapping him*) Not *you*! I'm talking about the royal pearl!

King Oh, yes! The pearl! (*To the audience*) Oh, you'll just love it! (*Going to the girl in the crowd*) And so will you! It's a real smasher! And you're a little smasher as well, aren't you!

He flirts with the girl and she gives a silly giggle

Queen Marmaduke!

King (*flinching*) Yes, dear?

Queen What *are* you doing?!

King Er . . . just on royal walkabout, dear.

Queen Well, *walkabout* over *here*!

King (*to the girl*) Must dash! (*He nods to the Queen*) His Master's voice! (*He scuttles to the Queen*) Yes, dear?

Queen You don't act a bit like a ruler!

King No, but I do a very good impression of a teapot! (*He does so and bursts with laughter*)

Queen (*slapping him*) I've half a mind——

King I know, dear!

Queen —to send you back to the Palace!

King Oh, goody-goody! (*To the audience*) I'll just be in time to watch (*TV programme*)!

Queen But, no! You will remain here and display your royal persona!

King (*with mock horror*) What in public, dear?

Queen (*slapping him*) Be quiet!

King (*to the audience, rubbing his arm*) Cor! I bet the Duke of Edinburgh doesn't get treated like this!

Queen (*to all*) On his recent travels abroad, our son, Prince Peter ... oh, where is he?

She looks around and sees Peter deep in conversation with Patience

(*To the King*) What is our son doing with that young person?

King A bit of all right by the look of it!

Queen Peter!

Peter (*to Patience*) Please excuse me. (*Coming down to the Queen*) Yes Mum?

Queen (*appalled*) Oh! How many times must I tell you, Peter. Don't call me Mum! It's so low-class! Call me Mother in public.

Peter (*teasing her*) Mother in public *what*?

King (*chipping in*) I don't know, but it's only at your *convenience*!

He and Peter laugh. The Queen is fuming with rage

Peter Look, you're giving Mum a royal *flush*!

They laugh again. The Queen drags the King to one side

Queen Speak to your son at once!

King (*waving to Peter*) Hallo, sonny!

Peter (*waving back*) Hallo, Daddy!

They roar with laughter

Queen (*with a haughty sniff*) Humph! It's easy to see who he takes after!

King (*going to Peter and putting his arm around him; to the audience*) Yes, he's just like me. Handsome an' debonair! Don't you think he's a smashin' bit of royal icing? Cop them legs! (*To someone*) I bet you wish you had a son with a figure like that, don't ya? You *don't*?! (*Worried*) No, I'm a bit worried about it myself!

Queen Enough of this shilly shallying! Tell them about the *pearl*!

Peter Oh, yes. (*To one and all*) During my recent travels abroad I was made a present of a fabulous pearl! It was a gift from the Mighty Sultan of Tichibum.

King (*to the audience*) A small royal seat!
Peter As well as being very beautiful to look at, the pearl is a priceless piece of precious perfection!
King (*to the audience*) Try sayin' that after you've had a few!
Peter In other words, our kingdom is now the richest in the land!
All Hurray!!
Queen And now—the pearl itself! Lord Chamberlain!

Graball, who has been lurking in the background until now, steps forward behind the King

Graball Majesty!
King (*jumping*) Yah! Cor! Right in the royal lug-'ole!
Queen Give me the casket.

Graball does so

Behold—the pearl! (*She is about to open the casket*)
King Wait! We're not all here yet! (*Looking around*) Where's my old friend, Dame Dimwit?
Dame (*off, in school*) Woo Hoo! Here I am! Coming!

Dame Dimwit enters from the school wearing an outrageous scholastic costume. Bertie and Gertie follow. Dame does a twirl

Bertie (*to the audience*) The Joan Collins of (*local place*)
King (*going to her*) Dame Dimwit!
Dame (*coyly*) Oh, Your Kingfulness!

Comic business as they bow and curtsy to each other and get into a mess

What a great *honour* this is! What a great *privilege* this is! What a great——
Bertie *Creep* this is!
Dame (*to Bertie*) Belt up! (*To the King, ultra posh*) How is one, Your Royalship?
King (*flirting*) All the better for seeing you, Dame dear!

Dame giggles coyly. The Queen coughs disapprovingly

(*To Dame*) I think the old woman's got a frog in her throat.

They giggle. The Queen coughs louder

Dame Now she's got a toad in the hole!

They fall about laughing

Queen Marmaduke!
King (*slinking back to her*) Yes, dear.
Queen (*to all, holding up the casket*) Men have fought, killed and died to possess the contents of this casket!
Bertie Wot's in it? Linda Lusardi's phone number?!
Queen (*opening the casket*) Behold! (*She takes out a large black pearl, the size of a snooker ball, and holds it up for all to see*)

*All react and come forward to gaze in wonderment at the pearl. Peter goes
back to Patience*

Bertie It's a snooker ball!

Gertie Yeah! I bet Steve Davis doesn't know you've got that!

Queen (*shocked and appalled*) A snooker ball!! I'll have you know, ignorant
child, that you are looking at the fabulous black pearl of Tichibum!

Gertie Pardon?

Queen Tichibum! Tichibum!

Gertie Ooo! Wash your mouth out!

Queen (*replacing the pearl and giving the casket to Graball*) And now our
royal presence is required elsewhere. We still have to visit other parts of
the town before returning to the Palace for the Royal Luncheon Party.
Peter! Marmaduke! We are leaving!

King (*waving to the crowd*) Ta ta, all! Bye! Bye! Have a nice day! (*To the
pretty girl*) Hope to see *you* again soon! (*Waving to the audience*) Cheerio,
folks! Don't do anything I wouldn't do! And I'd just like to say–

Queen (*bellowing at him*) We are leaving!

King (*to the audience, crestfallen*) We are leaving.

*He scuttles to her side. To suitable music, the King, Queen and Peter parade
around the stage and out through the gates, followed by the guards*

Graball sneaks to one side and remains out of the picture

*Waving and cheering, Dame, Bertie, Gertie, Patience and the crowd follow
the royal family out*

*As soon as the stage is empty, Graball sneaks to c and the stage darkens
slightly. Green spot on Graball*

Graball (*to the audience, with a villainous laugh*) Ha! Ha! Ha! Now that the
rubbishy royals are out of the way I can carry out me plan! Ha! Ha! (*He
looks around, opens the casket, takes out the pearl and gloats over it*)

Jack Horner enters from up R. *He sees Graball and hides behind a wall with
just his head sticking out*

(*To the pearl*) Soon you will be mine! All mine! (*To the audience*) I shall be
the richest man in the whole world when I steal this little beauty! Oh, yes,
I will!

"Oh, no, you won't" routine

I shall be so rich I'll be able to buy six houses in (*local well-to-do area*)!
Stealing it is going to be so easy! Ha! Ha! Ha! (*He puts the casket on the
ground and takes a fake pearl from his pouch*) See! A fake pearl! I place it in
the casket like *this*! (*He does so*) And I put the real pearl in my pouch, like
that! (*He does so*) Ha! By the time they discover the switch, if they ever do,
I shall be thousands of miles away! So simple and yet so clever! Don't you
think I'm clever?

"No!"

Well, who cares what you think anyway! You're just a miniscule mob of mindless morons! (*He picks up the casket*) Ha! Ha! Ha!

Jack What a crook!

Graball reacts. Jack disappears behind the wall

Graball (*looking around*) What! . . . What was that?! I . . . I thought I heard something! (*He turns back to the audience*) is there someone here?

Jack appears round the wall and signals the audience to say "No"

Tell me! Is there someone here?!

Audience No! No!

Graball Bah! I don't believe you! I'm going to look for myself!

Jack hides. Graball searches about the stage. He is just about to look behind Jack's wall when . . .

Peter enters through the gates

The spot on Graball goes out and the lighting returns to normal

Peter Lord Chamberlain!

Graball (*jumping with fright*) Ah! Er . . . Oh! Yes, Your Highness? (*He grovels*)

Peter What's delaying you? The Queen is very anxious about the pearl. You know she can't bear it out of her sight for more than five minutes.

Graball (*very smarmy*) Oh, it's quite safe, Your Highness. *Quite* safe with me.

Peter You'd better hurry and catch them up!

Graball Yes, Your Highness. At once, Your Highness.

With a sneer at the audience, he exits through the gates

Peter (*to the audience, with a shiver*) Brr! You know, that man gives me the creeps! He makes Dracula look like the Care Bears!

Jack rushes from hiding

Jack (*excitedly*) Your Highness! Your Highness! Something terrible has happened! . . . I . . . I——

Peter Calm down. What is it?

Jack I . . . I saw him! . . . The pearl! . . . He——

But the noisy entrance through the gates of Dame Dimwit, Bertie, Gertie, Patience and the children drown out his words

Dame (*going straight to Jack and taking him by the ear*) Little Jack Horner. Don't think I've forgotten about you. I promised you six of the best an' that's what you're goin' to get . . .

Jack (*protesting*) No, wait . . . Please . . . I must tell—

Dame Inside!

She pushes him into the school and exits. Bertie, Gertie and the children follow

Peter Well, Miss Patience, we meet again.

Patience Yes, Your Highness.

Peter I say, let's drop the formalities, shall we. Call me Peter. All my close friends do. And ... and I hope we're going to be close friends, Patience. (*He moves to her*)

Patience I'd like that very much ... Peter.

Peter I was hopeless at school. Always bottom of the class.

Patience Perhaps you didn't have the right teacher.

Peter How true. I'm sure if you'd been there I'd have been top every time. (*He moves closer*) I bet you're a wonderful teacher. In fact, you've taught me one lesson without realizing it. (*He takes her hands and sings*)

Song 5

A romantic duet with romantic lighting

> *After the song, we hear the unmistakable "Whack and wail" as Jack gets the last two strokes of the cane. Dame Dimwit enters from the school brandishing a broken cane*

Dame (*calling back into the school*) And let that be a lesson to you, Jack Horner! I'll cure you of your lateness and lies! Now, sit in the corner! (*With relish*) If you can! (*She turns and sees Peter*) Oh. Your Princeful-ness! (*Ultra posh*) Ho! Hi 'ad no hidea you wos still 'ere! (*She does an awkward curtsy*)

Peter That boy ... Jack Horner. He seemed to have something urgent to say to me.

Dame Oh, you don't want to listen to him, Your Royalship! He's always tellin' porkie pies ... er ... lies! Don't you bother about that young hooligan. I've got to the *bottom* of his problem! (*She swishes the broken cane*)

Peter Well, I'd better join the others. (*He takes Patience aside*) When can I see you again?

Dame follows them, all ears

Patience Whenever you like.

Peter I know! Be my guest at the Royal Luncheon Party today.

Dame (*pushing in*) Oh, Your Regalness! What an honour! I've never been to a Royal Beanfeast before!

Peter (*dumbfounded*) But, I didn't ask–

Dame Oh! How yummy! Oh I'm so looking forward to it!

Peter Well, I shall see you ... er ... both later. Goodbye.

He takes Patience's hand and kisses it. Dame holds out her hand, expecting the same

> *Peter just gives it a firm shake and exits through the gates*

Dame (*to the audience*) Humph! 'E never kissed *my* 'and! What's *she* got that I haven't got *more* of? (*To Patience*) Well, come along! We'd better go and get into our glad rags! Now, what shall I wear? I've got that nice little number I bought at (*local shop*)! Or perhaps I'll wear me tweed twin-set with matching mudguards! Come on, you can help me choose.

Dame and Patience exit R

Jack enters from the school, rubbing his painful rear and looking very downcast

Jack (*to the audience*) What am I going to do now, kids? I saw that crook of a Lord Chamberlain steal the pearl and no-one will listen to me! It's my own fault, I suppose. If only I hadn't made up all those excuses and told all those lies! But this time it really happened! You saw it happen, didn't you?

"*Yes.*"

Right! I won't give up! I must find someone who'll listen to me! I must! I must!

He exits DR, *still rubbing his sore bottom*

The school bell rings. Bertie, Gertie and the children charge out of the school, yelling and shouting

To suitable music, the Lights fade to Black-out

SCENE 2

A street

Tabs, or a frontcloth showing picturesque shops and houses

The King enters from DL, *and moves* C

King (*waving to the audience*) Watch'er me old subjects. Everything all right? Good! I've just managed to get away from the old woman for five minutes. What a woman! She's on at me all the time. Nag, nag, nag! (*To someone*) You know all about it, don't you, sir? Yes, I thought so! I can see the thumb-print on the top of your head! But I mustn't be too hard on my wife. She's got her good points—if she took off that crown you could see 'em! And she's no Kylie Minogue, is she? I'm not sayin' she's ugly, but I'd sooner take 'er with me than kiss 'er goodbye!

The pretty girl enters DR

(*To the audience*) Oh, I say! Look, it's my little friend again! Watch this! I'll give 'er a touch of the old Humphrey Gocarts! (*He sets his crown at a rakish angle and struts over to the girl*) Hi, doll!

The girl looks at him. He strikes a "macho" pose and gives her a flashing smile. She bursts into tears

(To the audience) Funny! It always works with the ladies at the *(local)* WI! *(To girl)* What's the matter my dear? Why the water-works?

Girl *(sniffing)* It's my boy-friend! He's ... he's going out with someone else! *(She wails loudly)* Waaa!!

King Cheer up, my dear. You'll soon find another boy-friend.

Girl I hate boys! I never want to see another boy again as long as I live! *(She stamps her foot)*

King Oh well ... er ... why not try an older man. *(With a twinkle)* Someone like me!

Girl You?

King Yes! Oh, there may be snow on the roof, but there's still a fire burnin' in the grate!

Song 6

A comedy duet and dance. After the number, the King shuts his eyes and puckers up his lips expecting a kiss from the girl

I'm ready, my little sugar-plum! *(He makes kissing noises)*

The Queen enters from DL *and stands watching with silent contempt*

The girl beats a hasty exit DR

(Feeling about and cooing) Where are yooo? *(He finds the Queen)* Ah! There you are! Ooh! You naughty little minx! Trying to hide from me, eh? *(He hugs the Queen and is puzzled)* I say! You seem to have grown a bit! Kiss! Kiss! *(He makes kissing noises)*

The Queen slaps him hard across the face ("slapstick" or cymbal crash). And he falls over

(Sitting up, dazed and overwhelmed. To the audience) Cor! What a kisser! I bet she drinks Carling Black Label! Phew!

Queen Marmaduke!

King *(still in a daze)* Yes, dear? ... *(He looks at the Queen, does a huge double-take and starts to crawl* R, *on his hands and knees)*

Queen Stop!

He freezes

Heel!

He turns and crawls to her

Sit!

He does so, dog-like with his hands held up like paws

King *(to the audience)* Look! I'm a royal corgi! *(He hangs out his tongue and starts panting)*

Queen Stand!

King What, no Bonio?

Queen *(booming)* I said stand!

King (*standing, then to the audience in a BBC voice*) And it's good-night from "One man and his dog". Next week you can see me win first prize at Crufts! (*He laughs with the audience*)

Queen (*slapping him*) Stop this nonsense at once! We must return to the Palace and prepare for the Royal Luncheon Party. I must speak to the Cook about the pigeon pie she's making.

King Pigeon pie? Does that mean you won't be giving me my usual today, dear?

Queen Your usual?

King Yes—tongue pie!

Fuming, the Queen chases him out DL

Jack Horner enters from DR, *looking down in the dumps*

Jack (*to the audience*) I still can't find anyone who'll listen to me. I try to tell them about the stolen pearl and they just tell me to push off and stop bothering them. There's only one thing for it! I'll go straight to the Royal Palace and see the King himself! (*He goes down* L, *stops and comes back*) Well, aren't you going to wish me good luck.

The audience shout "Good luck"

I can't hear you! Again!

They shout back

Thanks! I'll need it.

He waves and exits DL

Off R, *Bertie and Gertie are heard, yelling insults at each other*

Bertie (*off,* DR) Fatty!!
Gertie (*off,* DR) Skinny!!

They enter from down R

Bertie Droopy Drawers!!
Gertie Baggy Bum!!
Bertie Oh, go and take a long walk off a short pier!

Gertie pokes out her tongue, crosses her eyes and makes a hideous face at Bertie. He is unmoved. Gertie becomes aware of the audience, and returning her face to normal smiles sweetly at them. At this, Bertie reacts with mock horror

Ahhh! What a 'orrible face!! Cor! Ain't you ugly?! (*To the audience*) Ain't she ugly, kids?

Audience Yes!

Gertie (*to the audience*) No, I'm not! My mummy says I'm like a little angel that's fallen from the sky.

Bertie Yeah! What a pity you landed on yer face!

Gertie I 'ate you!

Bertie Tha's 'cos I'm cleverer than you. I've got a brain as big as a elephant!

Gertie Yeah! With ears to match! Well, I'm much cleverer than you! So there! (*She pokes out her tongue at him*)

Bertie Prove it!

Gertie I will! (*Stumped*) 'Ow?

Bertie By playin' ... (*with a flourish*) ta ra! The object identification game! (*To the audience*) We'll need your 'elp for this, folks! Will you 'elp? Well, you ain't got no choice, 'cos we've locked all the doors!

Gertie I'm not playin'! I'm shy! (*She strikes a shy pose*)

Bertie It's easy! I'll go down amongst the lovely layabouts and hold up some objects. All you've got to do is identify 'em ...

Gertie Tha's easy!

Bertie (*with fiendish glee*) Blindfolded! (*He whips out a large handkerchief and blindfolds the reluctant, squirming Gertie*) Now we'll see 'ow clever you are.

Gertie I don't wanna play this game. I wanna go 'ome.

Bertie Sher up! You've got the easy job! I've got to go down there!

The house lights come up and Bertie goes down into the audience. Gertie remains centre stage, a bundle of nerves. After a little byplay with the audience, Bertie selects a wrist-watch from someone

(*To the audience*) Now, don't give 'er any 'elp! (*Calling to Gertie*) Object number one comin' up! Are you nervous, Gertie?

Gertie (*shaking in her shoes*) N ... n ... no!

Bertie Have you got complete concentration?

Gertie 'Ave I got wot?

Bertie Concentration!

Gertie Not since Mummy gave me them little tablets.

Bertie Relax!

Gertie Yeah, I fink that's wot they was called.

Bertie Right then! 'Ere we go! Object number one! (*He holds up the watch*) Can you tell us what it is? (*Very pointedly*) Take your *time*, Gertie! Take your *time*!

Gertie goes into comic contortions as she concentrates hard

You ought to get it in a couple of *ticks*! A couple of *ticks*!

Gertie (*jumping up and down, excited*) I know! I know! It's a ... time bomb!

Bertie Wrong! Have another go! You're much too tense. Just *Rolex* a bit! *Rolex*!

Gertie (*jumping about*) I know! I know! It's ... a watch!

Bertie Correct! (*To the audience*) Give 'er a round of applause, folks!

The audience does so. Gertie bows and curtsies. Bertie returns the watch with comic asides, i.e. "You don't want this back, do you? Oh, you would!" etc. He moves on and selects the next object, a ladies' handkerchief. "I hope it's clean!" etc.

Gertie! Object number two! (*He holds up the handkerchief*) It's a very nice object. Not to be *sneezed* at!

Gertie goes into contortions again

I'm sure you *nose* wot it is, Gertie! *S'not* a difficult one at all! Well, *blow* me! She's taking a time, *blow* me, if she isn't!

Gertie (*jumping about*) I know! I know! It's ... a trumpet!

Bertie Wrong! We're all *hanker*-ing for you to tell us wot it is, Gertie! All *hanker*-ing!

Gertie (*jumping about*) I know! I know! It's ... a handkerchief!

Bertie Correct! (*To the audience*) Another round of claps, folks!

The audience applaud. Gertie curtsies again, Bertie returns the handkerchief and selects a pen from someone

Object number three! (*He holds up the pen*) This is an easy one, Gertie. You should get this one *right* first time!

Gertie goes into contortions

The lady/gentlemen I *biroed* this from doesn't think you're tryin' 'ard enough, Gertie!

Gertie I wanna go 'ome!

Bertie Come on, we're all de-*pen*-ding on you! Really de-*pen*-ding!

Gertie (*jumping about*) I know! I know! It's ... a pen!

Bertie Correct! (*To the audience*) Put yer 'ands together, folks!

The audience applaud and Gertie curtsies. Bertie returns the pen and moves on. He finds a man who is willing to remove his shoe. Bertie holds it far away and holds his nose. Comic business

Object number four! This is the *last* one, Gertie. You'll feel a right *heel* if you don't get it!

Gertie is in agonies of concentration

You're not tryin', Gertie! Put yer heart an' *sole* into it!

Gertie (*a despairing cry*) I wanna go 'ome!!

Bertie Oh, dear! There is a fly crawling up my sleeve! Go away, little fly! *Shoe!* ... *Shoe!* ...

Gertie (*jumping about*) I know! I know! It's ... a shoe!!

Bertie Correct! (*To the audience*) One last round of applause!

The audience applaud. Gertie removes the blindfold, curtsies and blows kisses. Bertie returns the shoe to its owner—"Will you wear it now or shall I wrap it?" He then returns to the stage and the house lights go down

Gertie (*to Bertie*) See! I was good! Wasn't I good?

Bertie Yeah! Good for nothin'! You were rubbish! (*To the audience*) What was she, kids?!

Audience Rubbish!

Gertie (*to the audience*) Oh, no I wasn't!

Bertie and Audience Oh, yes you were!

"Oh, no I wasn't!" "Oh, yes you were!" routine. It ends with Gertie having a tantrum and crying the place down. Bertie nonchalantly takes a paper bag of sweets from his pocket. Gertie sees this and the tantrum stops abruptly

Gertie Give us a sweetie!

He offers the bag. Gertie selects a sweet and chews it in happy, noisy bliss

Bertie Oh, you like the *green* ones, do you?
Gertie (*nodding and munching*) Mmm!
Bertie (*offering the bag*) 'Ave another green one. Take two.

Gertie does so and crams them into her mouth

You really do like them *green* ones, don't ya?
Gertie (*nodding and chewing*) Mmm! (*After a big swallow*) Don't you?
Bertie No—I always spit 'em back in the bag!

> *Gertie chokes and splutters. Bertie roars with laughter. Enraged, Gertie chases him out* DL *as ...*

The Lights fade to Black-out

SCENE 3

The Royal Palace

A sumptuous regal setting with pillars, chandeliers and rich tapestries, etc. Back c, *a grand staircase leads to a splendid archway with Palace/décor backing. Smaller archways down* R *and* L. *Across the* R *corner there is a dais with two thrones side by side. The one upstage is much the larger and is boldly inscribed "HERS". The smaller one is marked "HIS"*

The King and Queen are seated on their respective thrones. Both are now wearing red ermine-trimmed robes and larger crowns. The King's robe is much too long and he has a great deal of trouble with it. He has dozed off and keeps sagging against the Queen. Annoyed, she keeps pushing him away and trying to prop him upright. The luncheon guests are grouped about the stage. Prince Peter, magnificently attired, is leading the dancers in a stately gavotte, accompanied by singing

Song 7

After the number, all bow and curtsy to the King and Queen. She acknowledges them with a condescending clap. The King snores loudly

Queen (*digging him in the ribs*) Marmaduke!
King (*waking with a start*) What! ... Who! ... I ... I never touched her! ...
    It's all lies, I tell you! I ... (*He sees the guests*) Oh! What ho, you lot! (*He sees the audience and waves to them*) Halloee! (*To the Queen*) Look, dear!
    It's the (*local*) mob again!
Queen You were asleep! The throne is no place for sleeping!
King You're quite right, dear! There's a shockin' draught comes under that door, and ... Oh! You mean *this* throne? I thought you meant the ... (*He chuckles*) Oh, I am a silly old sovereign!

Queen (*rising, indignantly*) Oh! You're hopeless! (*She descends the dais*) I am going to the kitchen to supervize the cooking.

King (*to the audience*) She'll turn the milk sour!

Queen (*turning sharply*) *What* did you say?!

King Er ... I said, you do that, my little flower!

The Queen gives him a withering look and sweeps out L

Phew! That was a close one!

Graball enters through the C *archway and comes down the stairs in front of the dais*

Graball Your Majesty!

King (*to the audience*) Look out! Here comes the Black Adder! (*Or film TV nasty*) Yes, what is it, Lord Chamberlain?

Graball (*bowing*) Your Majesty, two female persons have arrived. They say they have been invited to the Royal Luncheon Party.

Peter That'll be Miss Patience and Dame Dimwit. I took the liberty of inviting them.

King Ho! Ho! That pretty young teacher, eh! You don't waste much time, my boy! (*To Graball*) Where are the ladies?

Graball They are waiting without.

King Without? Ho! Ho! We'll soon change *that*! Eh Peter, my boy. (*He winks at Peter. To Graball*) Well, don't just stand there like a black pudding on legs. Announce 'em!

Graball bows and goes up the stairs. The King preens himself

Graball (*at one side of the archway, announcing*) Miss Patience!

A fanfare is played. Patience, looking very pretty and charmingly dressed, enters and pauses in the archway. To suitable music, she descends the stairs

Peter goes forward to meet her and they bow and curtsy to each other. Peter leads her to the dais where she curtsies to the King. He jumps up and gives her a very low bow. He grips his back in agony and collapses on to the throne. Peter leads Patience to down L

(*Announcing*) Dame Drucilla Desdemona Delilah Dimwit, BA and public bar!

The fanfare is played. Dame Dimwit slinks on wearing an outrageous costume. She strikes a pose in the archway, then slowly comes down the stairs. "Colonel Bogey" is played loudly. Indignantly, Dame Dimwit stomps down to the front edge of the stage and stands with hands on hips glaring at the pianist or conductor. The music ends

Dame (*to pianist or conductor*) And the same to you, with pizzicatos on!

King (*rising and coming down to Dame*) I say! Dame dear, you're looking very chic!

Dame (*holding out her dress*) What this old rag! Oh, it's just a little something I ran up during a woodwork class! It's called the bingo look!

King Why?

Dame Eyes down for a full house! (*She throws out her chest*)

She and the King fall about laughing

The guests and dancers drift off R

Graball comes down the stairs and moves DR

Peter Dad, I'd like to show Patience around the Palace.

King Certainly, my boy! Dame Dimwit can stay and chat with me. (*To Dame*) Would you care for a little tête-à-tête?

Dame Oh, how kind! But couldn't you make it a double with a picked onion in it?

Peter leads Patience out down L

King (*sidling up to Dame*) Would you care to see my hangings?

Dame (*aghast*) Eh?!!

King The Royal Tapestries.

Dame Oh!

The King leads her upstage and points out the tapestries. While their backs are turned, Graball speaks to the audience. The stage darkens slightly. Spot on Graball

Graball As soon as night falls I will leave this tinpot kingdom forever! I'll go abroad, sell the pearl and live a life of luxury! No longer will I be a servant! No more taking orders! *I* will be the master and everyone else will be my slaves! (*He forgets himself and laughs demonically*) Ha! Ha! Ha! Ha!

Dame Dimwit and the King react and turn around. The spot on Graball goes out and the lighting returns to normal

Dame What's up with Edwina Currie over there?

King (*moving to Graball*) Are you all right, Lord Chamberlain?

Graball (*regaining control*) I ... I beg Your Majesty's pardon. I was coughing. (*He gives a polite cough*) I have a slight chest cold.

King Sorry to hear that. I know an excellent remedy. You must rub your chest with VICK. (*To Dame*) Isn't that right, Dame Dimwit?

Dame (*who has been gazing about and not listening*) Beg your pardon, Your Royal Puddin'?

King Rub your chest with VICK!

Dame (*puzzled but game for anything*) Er ... well, if you insist! Where is he? (*She calls off*) Vic! *Vic!* Where are you?! *Victor!*

The King roars with laughter. The Dame is bewildered, but laughs just the same

Graball (*aside to the audience*) What a pair of wallies!

He bows to the King and exits down R

Dame (*shivering*) Ugh! How do you put up with that slippery slice of slime! He gives me goose-pimples on me goose-pimples!

King Don't let's talk about him. Let's talk about—(*he sidles up to her*) *you*!
Dame (*acting coy*) Oooh, Your Imperial Leather!

A commotion is heard off-stage, back C

Guard (*off*) Hey! Come back! You can't go in there!

> *Jack Horner bursts in through the archway and runs down the stairs. He is hotly pursued by the guard*

Jack (*running straight to the King*) Your Majesty! Your Majesty!
Dame Jack Horner!
Jack Your Majesty, I *must* speak to you!
Dame (*grabbing Jack by the ear*) How dare you burst in here like a Rambo on an off-day! Whatever will his Majesty think!
Jack (*to the King*) I have something very important to tell you—
Dame (*twisting his ear*) Silence, Jack Horner! Back to school this instant and prepare for afternoon lessons! (*To the King*) He'll do anything to get out of going to school!
Jack Please, Your Majesty, I must tell you—
Dame (*to the guard*) Colonel—*kick 'im out*!

The guard hauls the protesting Jack away and up the stairs

Jack (*as he goes*) No! Wait! You *must* listen to me! ... Your Majesty! ... Please let me tell—

He is dragged out by the guard

King (*impressed*) I must say, Dame, you're very firm.
Dame Well, it's this new girdle I'm wearing. It's ... oh! Silly me! I see what you mean! Oh, yes! I don't take any nonsense from my pupils. I'm a great believer in putting my hand down with a firm foot!

Peter and Patience enter from down L

Oh, look! Scott and Charlene (*or other romantic duo*) are back!
King (*to Patience*) Well, my dear, what do you think of our little Palace?
Patience It's marvellous—so many beautiful rooms!
King And which room do you like the best?
Patience Oh, I think the music room is my favourite.
King Ah, yes! It's much better since we had the plumbing fixed and the new chain fitted ...
Peter (*amused*) Not *that* music room, Dad, the *music* music room!
King Oh! (*He chuckles*) Are you interested in music, my dear?
Patience I love it. I teach it at the school. Singing is my forte.
Dame (*pushing in, not wanting to be left out*) I do a bit of warbling myself, Your Royalness! My voice has been much admired. Someone once said I sounded like Vera Lynn.
King (*aside to the audience*) More like Vera Duckworth, I'll bet! (*To Dame*) What type of voice have you got?
Dame Well, sometimes I have a falsetto voice ...

King That's funny! My wife has a falsetto teeth! (*He roars with laughter. To Dame*) Do you sing in duets?

Dame No, in the *bath* mostly.

King (*very enthusiastic*) Oh, I say! You make me feel like bursting forth myself!

Dame Well, don't do it over *me*!

Song 8

A comic-quartet, involving the audience if desired. Peter and Patience maintain the singing while Dame Dimwit and the King enjoy themselves with comic business and tomfoolery. Half-way through, Dame Dimwit stops the others and addresses the pianist or conductor

Whoa! Stop! Mr/Mrs Lloyd Webber! You're not playin' it right! Oh, look! No wonder! (*To the audience*) He's/She's got the little black dots upside down! (*To pianist/conductor*) Now do it properly!

They continue and finish the song. Dame and King bow, curtsy and blow kisses to the audience like opera stars. The Dame does a low curtsy and falls over dragging the King down on top of her

At that moment the Queen sweeps on from R. *Two guards follow her, one carries the pearl casket. The guests enter from* R *and* L *Graball enters* L

Queen Marmaduke!

The King reacts and pretends to be examining the carpet

King (*to Dame*) And it's got a lovely pile! Just feel it.

He and Dame feel the floor

Queen Get up!
King Yes, dear.

He and Dame disentangle themselves and stand up

Queen (*moving to* C) Attention everyone! Before we go into luncheon, I am going to allow you another chance to feast your eyes on our fabulous pearl!

General delight. Unseen, Graball pats his pouch and sneers. The Queen motions to the guard who comes forward and opens the casket for her. The Queen takes out the pearl and proudly holds it aloft for all to see. General excitement

Peter (*alarmed and going quickly to the Queen*) Mother!
Queen What on earth's the matter, Peter?!
Peter Give it to me! (*He snatches the pearl from the astounded Queen and examines it very closely*)

General bewilderment

I thought so! This is a fake!

General sensation. Graball edges slowly to the exit down L

Queen A fake?! (*With dread*) You don't mean—
Peter Yes! The real pearl has been stolen!

Uproar. The Queen is struck dumb with horror

King Sufferin' sceptres! Are you sure, Peter?
Peter I carried the real pearl all the way back from the Sultan's Palace! I had it with me for months! Believe me, *this* is a fake!
Queen (*finding her voice and letting out a scream*) Ahhh!! Marmaduke! Do something! Do something!!
King (*running up and down in a panic*) Yes, dear! ... Yes, dear! ... (*Stopping*) What?
Queen (*wailing*) Oo! Our fabulous pearl! Gone! Stolen! Oo! (*Rounding on the King*) This is all *your* fault!
King (*to the audience*) I thought it would be!
Peter The pearl has been closely guarded ever since I brought it home. The only time the switch could have been made was when we showed it around the town this morning! (*Suddenly turning to Graball*) Lord Chamberlain!
Graball (*turning with a start*) Er ... yes, Your Highness?
Peter Was the pearl ever out of your sight?
Graball No, Highness! I guarded it with my life!
Queen Oh, what is to be done! My pearl! My lovely, priceless pearl!
Peter (*to all*) A search must be made throughout the entire Kingdom! The Royal Pearl and its thief must be found at once! (*Going to Graball*) Lord Chamberlain, I shall need your help! Come with me! (*To guards*) Men!

Peter, Graball and the guards exit up the stairs. The guests, in great excitement, exit R *and* L

Dame (*to the Queen*) Does this mean we won't be gettin' any grub?

The Queen just lets out a despairing wail

Dame Dimwit reacts and makes a quick exit, followed by Patience

Queen (*staggering about, weakly*) Oh! All this has been too much for me! I ... I think I'm going to faint! (*To the King, anything but weakly*) Marmaduke! Catch me! Ooo!

She faints into the King's arms. He staggers under her weight and with much puffing and blowing lowers her to the floor. He makes sure she is unconscious, then does a few karate chops in her direction

King (*to the audience*) Shh! Don't wake her up! Now I can get a bit of peace and quiet.

He tip-toes to his throne and sits. He gets into a comfortable position and goes to sleep as the Lights fade to Black-out

SCENE 4

The street again

Tabs, or the frontcloth used in Scene 2

Peter enters DL, followed by two guards

Peter (*annoyed, calling off* L) Lord Chamberlain!

Graball enters DL, followed by two guards

Graball Yes, Your Highness?

Peter Would it be too much trouble to ask you to keep up? This isn't a Sunday afternoon stroll in the park, you know!

Graball I'm sorry, Highness, but searching all those houses has quite fatigued me. Can't I take a little rest and catch you up later?

Peter No, you can't! I'll search (*local*) road. (*He points* R) You take (*local*) street. (*He points* L) The pearl must be found! We'll meet back here. Men!

Peter and the two guards exit DR

Graball (*to the guards*) Well, don't just stand there like a couple of sticks of rock! You heard the Prince, the pearl must be found! Get searching! I'll join you later. Move! *Move!*

The guards give him a dirty look and exit

The stage darkens. A green spot comes up on Graball

(*to the audience*) Ha! Ha! Ha! What a numbskull that Royal Nincompoop is! Little does he know that the pearl is right under his stupid, stuck-up nose! (*He pats his pouch and gives a gloating laugh*) Now that the coast is clear I'm going to make me getaway! I'm leaving right now! Farewell, puny peasants! I can't say it's been a pleasure knowing you! Ha! Ha! Ha!

The lighting returns to normal. He goes to exit DR, but ...

Rosa enters and blocks his path. She is a pretty gypsy girl, carrying a basket with pegs, heather, ribbons etc.

Rosa Good-day, fine gentlemen. Buy something from a poor gypsy girl. (*Showing her wares*) Pretty pegs—happy heather—cheap charms—ravishing ribbons. Buy something and get lucky.

Graball Stand aside! How dare you hinder me, you impertinent, dirty little ragamuffin!

Rosa (*getting her dander up*) Hey! Who do you think you're talking to! Just because I'm a gypsy there's no need to call me names! Besides, you're no Jason Donovan (*or other romantic hero*) yerself!

Graball (*trying to get past her*) Out of my way!

Rosa keeps in front of him

Bah! If you don't let me pass, I'll ... (*He raises his fist*)

Rosa (*throwing down her basket*) You'll *what*?!! (*She puts up her fists and* *forces him backwards)* Go on, try it! I'll give ya a knuckle sandwich! You big black bag of wind. (*Making play with her fist*) Come on, then! Come on!

Graball cowers away

Peter enters from DR, followed by the guards

Peter Lord Chamberlain! What's going on here!
Rosa (*to Peter, indicating Graball*) Does *that* belong to you?
Peter Well ... in a manner of speaking.
Rosa If it belonged to *me* I'd have it put down!
Peter Lord Chamberlain, I thought I told you to search that street.
Graball I was about to, Highness, when this little—

Rosa takes a threatening step towards him

Er ... person detained me.
Rosa I was only trying to make a living. (*She picks up her basket. To Peter*) Care to buy something, Your Highness. Special rate for Royals.

The two guards enter from down L

Peter (*to them*) Any luck, men?
Guards No, Your Highness.
Peter (*with a sigh*) We drew a blank as well!

Jack Horner enters DR, sees the Prince and rushes to him

Jack Your Highness! You've got to listen to me! I know who—
Peter (*suddenly struck by a thought and ignoring Jack completely*) The Town Hall! We haven't searched there! Lord Chamberlain! Men! Follow me!

He rushes out DL, followed by Graball and the guards

Jack (*running to the exit and calling after Peter*) Wait ... Your Highness! ... Please ... (*He turns back, dejected*) Oh, drat! It's hopeless!
Rosa (*putting down her basket and moving over*) What's the matter?
Jack (*turning, surprised to see her there*) Oh ... Who are you?
Rosa I'm Rosa.
Jack Hallo, Rosa. Pleased to meet you. I'm Jack—Jack Horner. Are you a gypsy?
Rosa No, I'm Indiana Jones! Am I a gypsy he asks! Who else but a gypsy would be dressed like this?
Jack I ... I didn't mean to be rude. (*Moving closer*) I'm sorry—Rosa.
Rosa There's no need to be—Jack.
Jack (*to the audience*) She's nice!
Rosa You seemed very upset just now. What's wrong?
Jack It's about the Royal Pearl!
Rosa It's been stolen hasn't it?
Jack Yes, and I know who stole it! I saw him with my own eyes! It was the Lord Chamberlain!
Rosa What, old black magic?

Jack Yes! If something isn't done soon he'll do a runner with it. I've tried and tried to tell them, but no-one will listen to me. (*With a sigh*) Still! With my reputation as a liar what else can I expect!

Rosa I wish there was something I could do to help you.

Jack (*overjoyed and taking her hands*) Does that mean you believe me, Rosa? You don't think I'm just making the whole thing up?

Rosa Of course I believe you. We gypsies have special powers. We can look into people's eyes and see what's in their hearts. (*Gazing into his eyes*) I can see you're telling the truth.

Jack (*drawing her closer*) And what else can you see?

Song 9

A bashful romantic song and dance. After the song, Jack and Rosa are about to kiss when . . .

> *Meg an old gypsy woman, enters* DR, *carrying a basket*

Meg Rosa!

Rosa (*turning to her, but still embracing Jack*) Meg! This is Jack Horner. He has a problem.

Meg It doesn't look much like it from where I'm standing! Come, Rosa. It's time we returned to our camp. Vasaleno will be waiting to count the money we've collected.

Rosa (*to Jack*) Vasaleno is our chief . . . a lovely man . . . (*With great disgust*) If you like rats!

Meg Hush, child! (*She picks up Rosa's basket*) Take your basket and let us be on our way.

Rosa But Jack needs help! The Royal Pearl has been stolen! He saw it done but no-one will listen to him!

Meg That's no concern of ours.

Rosa Isn't there anything we can do to help him?

Meg Child, we are gypsies. Social outcasts, driven from one place to another. Who is going to listen to anything a gypsy has to say! Come, we must be going. (*She moves to the down* R *exit*)

Rosa But—

Meg (*firmly*) Rosa, do as I say!

Rosa Don't worry, Jack, I know everything will turn out right in the end.

> *She hurriedly kisses Jack on the cheek, and exits with Meg,* DR

Jack (*to the audience*) Coo! She kissed me! I'll never wash that cheek again! What do you think of that, boys! I bet you wish she'd kissed you!

Audience reaction

> It's not soppy, it's nice! Well, I liked it, so there! (*He moves* L)

> *Peter, Graball and the guards enter from* DR

Peter Another fruitless search! I hate to admit it, but it looks as if the thief's got away with the pearl!

Graball Very sad! (*He shakes his head sadly, then, unseen, he sneers at the audience*)
Jack (*rushing to Peter*) Your Highness!
Peter (*wearily*) Oh not *you* again!
Jack I must tell you something!
Peter (*resigned*) Very well. What is it?
Jack (*to the audience*) At last! (*To Peter*) It's about the pearl! I know who—
Queen (*calling, off* L) Peter!

She sweeps on from DL, *very agitated*

Peter! (*She goes to Peter, pushing Jack into the background*) Have you found it? Have you found my pearl?!
Peter I'm afraid not, Mother. We've searched everywhere! Even (*well-known local character*)'s place! It's just vanished into thin air.
Queen Oh! This is horrible! horrible! (*She calls off* L) Marmaduke!

The King enters, unconcerned, DL. *He is eating jelly babies from a paper bag*

King (*to the audience*) What ho, folks!
Queen What have you been doing?
King Buyin' jelly babies dear! (*He offers the bag*) Want one?
Queen (*appalled*) Oh! How can you think of sweets at a time like this! Our fabulous pearl has been stolen and all you can do is fill your face with jelly babies! Haven't you got any priorities?!
King No dear, only jelly babies! (*He laughs and eats*)
Jack (*pushing in; to the Queen*) Your Majesty!
Queen Who are *you*?
Jack Jack Horner, Your Majesty. Please let me speak to you! I—
Queen Go away, boy! Why aren't you at school?! Go to school immediately!
Jack But—
Queen (*booming and pointing off* L) To school! Go!!

Jack shrugs, and exits dejectedly down L

Peter The *school*! We haven't searched Dame Dimwit's school!
Queen We will do so at once! Marmaduke!

She sweeps out DL, *followed by Peter, Graball, and the guards*

When they have gone the King starts throwing out sweets to the audience

Queen (*booming, off* L) Marmaduke!!
King (*calling back, sweetly*) Coming, my dearest!

He pokes out his tongue in her direction, throws out a few more sweets then scampers out DL, *waving to the audience, as . . .*

The Lights fade to Black-out

Scene 5

The backcloth and wings show a comic scholastic muddle with bulging bookshelves, globes, maps, letters of the alphabet, children's drawings, etc. There is a table back C, with cookery lesson equipment on it, bowls of "crazy foam", flour shakers, rolling pins, etc. A smaller table is set against the R wings. Against the L wings is a large "Heath Robinson" style oven with practical door. A stage cloth is advisable for this scene

Dame Dimwit, in comic cookery attire, stands near the table R. The children, singing and dancing, each take a pie from the oven and place it on the table R, for Dame Dimwit's inspection. During this, Bertie and Gertie are trying to claim one of the pies, but without success. All wear small chef hats and aprons. Bertie and Gertie's are outsize and comic

Song 10

After the number, Bertie and Gertie start to creep out down L

Dame Just a minute, you two!

They freeze

I haven't seen your pies yet! (*She moves* C) Where are they?

Bertie and Gertie go to the oven and bring out two hideous, burnt offerings! (Still smoking, if possible) They take them to Dame Dimwit who reacts with horror

And what, my little Delia Smiths, do you call these?!
Bertie À la carte, miss!
Dame Well, I don't know about *à la*, but you're both in the *carte*!
Gertie (*starting to wail*) I wanna go 'ome!
Dame I've never seen anything so disgusting! It's obvious you weren't paying attention during the cookery lesson! Very well! You can both do it all again! (*To the children*) The rest of the class can go out to play!

The children exit UL

There follows a slapstick cookery scene for Dame Dimwit, Bertie and Gertie. See Production Notes. To end, Bertie and Gertie say to the audience "And here's one I made earlier". From under the table they produce two perfect uncooked pies and put them in the oven

The Queen sweeps on from R, followed by Peter, the King, Graball and the guards. Patience and the children enter UL and fill the back of the stage

(*Flustered*) Oh! Your Royal Jellies! Please forgive the mess, but you've caught me all of a do-da!
Queen Dame Dimwit, as you know, the royal pearl has been stolen! A search of your school, and everyone in it, must be carried out immediately!

Dame (*gushing*) Oh, my quarters are wide open to you! Please search every crook and nanny!

Peter (*to the guards*) Men!

The guards go upstage and search Patience and the children. Downstage, Peter and the King search Bertie and Gertie. Comic business with them finding all sorts of comic odds and ends, strings of sausages, rubber fish, etc., etc.

(*To the Queen*) No pearl! (*To the guards*) Men?

Guard Nothing, Your Highness.

Dame (*coughing politely*) Ah hem! You've forgot little me! I haven't been given the once over yet! (*Holding out her arms*) Who's going to search *moi*?

The King moves eagerly towards her, but the Queen pushes him back

Queen The Lord Chamberlain shall attend to it.

Dame (*to the audience, disgusted*) Just my luck to get old Black an' Decker! (*As Graball approaches her*) I hope you've washed your hands!

He searches her. She is ticklish. Comic business and ad libs

Oooo! Ha! Ha! Oh, don't touch what you can't afford! Oh, not there! Oo! I'll give you twenty-four hours to stop that! . . . etc. (*To end*) Am I clean?

Graball That's about *all* you are!

Dame (*advancing on Graball*) Now, it's *your* turn!

Graball (*backing off*) What!!

Dame Why not? You're not one of the Royals! You're just a jumped-up flunkey!

Peter Dame Dimwit is right. It's only fair that you should be searched as well, Lord Chamberlain. We must show no favouritism.

Graball (*to the Queen, desperate now*) But, Your Majesty—

Queen Silence! You will be searched!

Graball (*thinking quick and bowing*) Certainly, Your Majesty, but may I suggest that the palace guards be searched first.

Queen So be it!

Peter (*to the guards*) Men!

The guards form a line on stage L, and are searched by Peter and the King. All the others group around them and watch closely. Graball moves away to DR. Unseen, he slips the pearl from his pouch

Graball (*to the audience*) Curse upon curse! I must hide the pearl! But where?! (*He looks about desperately then sees the pies on the table R and goes up to it*) Ah. The very place! I'll hide it inside one of these pies and come back for it later!

Jack Horner enters DR, and, unobserved, watches as . . .

Graball lifts the crust on one of the pies and puts the pearl inside. This done, he joins the others. Jack goes to the table and takes the pearl from the pie. Bertie and Gertie look across and see him

Bertie } (*together, yelling and pointing to Jack*) Look!!
Gertie }

All turn and see Jack holding the pearl. General uproar

Queen Arrest that boy!

Two of the guards rush over and grab the confused Jack. They haul him before the Queen

(*Snatching the pearl from Jack*) Give me that!
Graball (*aside*) Curse the meddling brat!
Dame (*appalled*) Oh, Jack Horner! You're a disgrace to the school!
Jack It wasn't me! I'm innocent! It wasn't—
Queen Away with him! Lock him in the deepest dungeon!

The guards begin to drag Jack out DR

Jack (*as he goes*) I'm innocent! ... Let me explain! ... It wasn't me! ... It was—

Jack is dragged off. The Queen, Peter and the guards follow them out

Dame Dimwit is making the most of the situation and is being soothed by the King, Patience and the children

Graball (*to the audience*) Bah! That wretched Jack Horner! Now I'll have to steal the pearl all over again! But, fear not, I shall not fail a second time! Ha! Ha! Ha!

He exits DR

Dame (*over the top*) Oh, the shame. Oh, the disgrace! To think, I was 'arbourin' a criminal in my school! (*Pleading to the King*) Oh, don't give me the sack, Kingy! I'm too old to get another job! (*She cries on his shoulder*) Boo hoo!
King (*patting her*) There—there! Diddums! Don't take on so. I'm not blaming you, Dame dear.
Dame (*all tears and misery vanish*) You're not? Great! (*To Bertie and Gertie*) Now then, it's time to see how your pies are doin'! His Majesty can have the first slice!

The children sing a reprise of Song 10. Bertie and Gertie open the oven door and invite the King and Dame Dimwit to look. They both peer right inside. The oven explodes with a tremendous bang! Flashes and clouds of smoke! With "crazy foam" plastered faces, Dame Dimwit and the King are thrown backwards, stagger about and fall over. On the last note of music—

CURTAIN

ACT II

SCENE 1

The Gypsy camp in the woods

Prominent on stage R, *is a large, brighly painted caravan with a practical door and steps up to it. Smaller caravans are half seen in the background. There is a camp fire with a cooking pot and several painted barrels and boxes. The backcloth and wings show the woods*

The scene is alive with colour, music and movement. Several gypsies are discovered dancing a wild gypsy dance with tambourines. Others are grouped about, singing and clapping in time with the music. Seated on a barrel near the large caravan is Vasaleno, the gypsy chief. He is a fat, loud, sleazy individual, eating a huge chicken drumstick. Bopo, a comical little fellow, is seated on the ground near Vasaleno's barrel

Song 11

The song and dance ends with wild applause from the spectators, and they gather around the dancers with noisy congratulations

Unseen by the gypsies, Jack runs on from DL. *He pauses* C *to get his breath, then runs out* DR

Vasaleno (*roaring at the gypsies*) Enough!! Shuta your faces!

All go silent and clear L. *Vasaleno throws the drumstick over his shoulder and, removing Bopo's hat, wipes his fingers in his hair*

Now we 'ave ze singin'! Who is gonna sing Vasaleno ze song, huh?

No-one volunteers. With an angry roar, Vasaleno jumps down from his barrel and strides over to the gypsies

Wota matter for you? You no 'ear good! You all got clothes pegs in your ear 'oles! Vasaleno, king of all ze gypsies wanta ze song! (*He points to a gypsy*) You sing!

The gypsy shakes his head and shrinks away

(*To another*) You!

She hides behind another. During this, Bopo is slowly crawling, on all fours, towards the exit DR. *Vasaleno sees him and gives a roar*

Hey!

Bopo freezes in mid-crawl

Where you go? Come 'ere!

Bopo crawls back to Vasaleno and cat-like rubs against his legs and purrs loudly. Vasaleno reacts and kicks Bopo over

Ahh! Stopa that stuff! (*He hauls Bopo to his feet*) You singa for me, huh! You sing good or . . . (*He whips out an ugly dagger and holds it against Bopo's belly*) I cuta your tripes out! Sing!

Bopo gulps, smiles nervously, then does a short comic send-up of an up-to-date pop song. All react and put their fingers in their ears

Bopo (*beaming at Vasaleno*) You like? That's 'ow zay sing on topa-ze popies every Thursday night.

Vasaleno (*grabbing him*) Ahh! You calla dat singin'. It sound like (*pop singer/group*) with 'is tonsils toasted! You no take the Mickey Mouse of Vasaleno. For zat, I cuta off your noses!

He holds his dagger up to Bopo's face. Bopo shivers and shakes with fright

Rosa and Meg enter from DL

Bopo 'Ere come Rosa! . . . *She* sing for you! . . . Rosa sing pretty! . . . You ask!

Vasaleno (*throwing Bopo from him and striding to Rosa*) You sing for me— now!

Rosa (*defiant, with hands on hips*) Why should I?

Vasaleno Wot!! You no question de word of Vasaleno, king of all ze gypsies! I say you sing, you *sing*!

Rosa (*facing front with folded arms*) Oh, go and play with your crystal balls!

Vasaleno explodes with rage. Bopo doubles up with laughter and Vasaleno kicks him in the pants

Vasaleno (*to Rosa, fuming*) Ahhgr! For that I cuta off your leetle nose! I cuta off your leetle ears! I cuta off your leetle everythin's! (*He advances on her, brandishing his dagger*)

Rosa (*whipping out her own small dagger and thrusting it in Vasaleno's face*) Just try it, Fatso!

Vasaleno backs off, very scared. Rosa makes a sudden lurch at him, and, yelling with fright, he runs into the large caravan, slamming the door behind him. Rosa roars with laughter and all the gypsies join in

Now that old windbag's out of the way, I *will* sing! We'll *all* sing!

Song 12

A jolly song and dance for Rosa, Bopo and the gypsies

After the song, Rosa and Meg move upstage and exit

The gypsies disperse about the stage. The door of the caravan opens slowly and Vasaleno peeps out. He makes sure Rosa is nowhere to be seen, then makes a "macho" entrance, cuffing Bopo for good measure

Peter enters L, *followed by two guards*

Peter Good-day to you, gypsies! Is your leader here?

Vasaleno (*striding to* C) I am 'e! I am Vasaleno, king of all ze gypsies! Who is you, huh?

Peter Prince Peter of Pantomania.

Bopo does an exaggerated bow, and Vasaleno cuffs him

Vasaleno Stopa that stuff! 'E *only* a prince! (*He slaps his chest*) I, *king*! (*To Peter*) Wota you wants?

Peter We are looking for a runaway thief. He is a boy called Jack Horner. He managed to escape while being taken to the Palace dungeon. We chased him into these woods and lost track of him. Have you seen a boy? Has he been this way?

Vasaleno I ain't seen no boy! I 'ate all boys—an' girls! (*To the audience*) I eata zem for breakfast!

He snarls at the audience. Bopo tries to copy him but fails, and ends up giggling. Vasaleno cuffs him

Peter There is a reward for his capture. Two hundred gold pieces.

Vasaleno (*drooling and rubbing his hands*) Two 'undred gold pieces! You want zis boy alive, or ... (*He makes grisly throat-slitting gestures*)

Peter Alive! He must be given a fair trial!

Vasaleno (*to the audience*) Pah! Wota spoilsport!

Peter So keep your eyes peeled. Good-day.

He exits, DR, followed by the guards

Vasaleno Ho! Ho! Two 'undred gold pieces! Taxa free! (*To gypsies*) My tribe! Into ze woods an' find me zis Jack 'Orner! An' remember, who ever catch 'im, *I* get ze reward! No double cross, or I cuta your tripes out! *Go*!!

The gypsies exit in all directions

Bopo is about to follow

Vasaleno Hey. Where you go?

Bopo I go find Jack 'Ornet!

Vasaleno You stay 'ere an' guard ze camp!

Bopo salutes him and marches up and down in comic sentry fashion

(*To the audience*) 'E bigger plonker zan you lot!!

He exits UR

As soon as he is out of sight, Bopo searches for the discarded drum-stick. He finds it, and chewing happily, exits behind the large caravan

A slight pause, then Rosa creeps on from DR, and looks about

Rosa (*calling off* R) It's all right, Jack. There's no-one here.

Jack enters DR and moves C

Jack Oh, Rosa, I'm in a right mess! It was bad enough everyone thinking me a liar, but now everyone thinks I'm a thief as well!

Rosa Not *everyone*, Jack. I still believe in you—and I'm going to help.

Jack (*taking her hand*) You mustn't! It's better you have nothing more to do with me. You'll get into terrible trouble aiding and abetting a criminal on the run.

Rosa But you're not a criminal. You didn't steal the pearl!

Jack *You* know that, and so do I—(*he indicates the audience*)—and so do *they*! But, it's hopeless! The only thing I can do is keep running and hope they never find me.

Rosa Then I will run away with you.

Jack No. I think too much of you, Rosa, to let you spend the rest of your life like a hunted animal. I must go it alone.

Rosa (*near to tears*) Oh, Jack!

They embrace

Bopo, still chewing the drumstick, emerges from behind the caravan. On seeing the couple, he stops in mid-chew, then comes down to them

Bopo (*brightly*) 'Ello!

Startled, Rosa and Jack part

Rosa Er ... Hallo, Bopo ... (*Indicating Jack, at a loss*) This is ... er ...

Jack takes charge of the situation and strides to Bopo in a devil-may-care manner. (Note—Jack assumes an Australian accent for the following dialogue, à la "Neighbours". If the actor/actress is unhappy with that particular accent another can be substituted i.e.—cockney for "East Enders", Northern for "Coronation Street", American for "Dallas", etc. The necessary changes in the dialogue to accommodate the soap opera chosen will need to be made accordingly)

Jack (*vigorously shaking Bopo's hand*) G'day, sport! Ramsey's the name! Rosa's cousin from Down Under!

Bopo (*puzzled, looking at the ground*) Down under?

Jack S'right! You know, me old cobber!—Croc Dundee—Dame Edna ...

Bopo (*catching on*) Ah. (*He sings or "la-las" the theme music to "Neighbours"*)

Jack Good on ya, cobber! I'm over here on a flyin' visit! Came with the flyin' doctor, in fact!

Bopo Hey! I was tinkin' you wos zis Jack 'Orner they all lookin' for.

Jack Jack Horner! Strewth, no! Wouldn't have anythin' to do with that dingo! I don't give a Castlemaine XXXX about his sort. Well, it's time I packed me didgeridoo in me tucker bag and left for the Billabong! (*He slaps Bopo on the back*) So long, me old cobber! (*To Rosa*) So long, Rosa, me old Sheila.

He kisses Rosa on the cheek and makes for the exit DR. *Rosa runs after him*

Rosa Wait ... !

Jack (*whispering to her, as himself*) Don't worry about me. I'll stay hidden until dark and then make my getaway.

Rosa But, Jack . . .

Jack Try to forget all about me, Rosa. I'm bad news. Goodbye. (*Aloud to Bopo*) S'long, sport!

Bopo (*waving*) S'long, me old cobblers! Say 'allo to Mrs Mangel for me!

Jack exits DR

Rosa bursts into tears. Bopo tries to comfort her

Hey, you no cry, Rosa. 'E come back up from down under soon. No cry, huh? Hey. I got somethin' that cheer you up!

He runs out L *and returns, leading a quaint little pony*

(*Bringing pony to* C) 'Ere 'e is! 'E called Pedro! Come, Rosa, say 'allo to Pedro.

Rosa dries her tears, and moving to Pedro, finds him irresistible

Rosa (*stroking his neck*) Hallo, Pedro.

Pedro lovingly nuzzles his head into Rosa

Bopo See! 'E like you! Pedro like everyone! Everyone except—you know who! (*He does an impersonation of Vasaleno*)

Rosa Vasaleno?

On hearing that name, Pedro whinnies, thrashes his head from side to side, kicks his legs and generally goes berserk. Comic business as Bopo calms him down

Bopo (*to Rosa*) Shh! You no say 'is name in front of Pedro. (*To Pedro*) You no like that ugly, fat man, huh?

Pedro shakes his head and stamps the ground

Pedro go crazy if 'e 'ear 'is name, an' when 'e see 'im . . .

Vasaleno strides on from DR

Pedro sees him, and going berserk, charges at him

Vasaleno yells in fright and runs out DR

Bopo restrains Pedro and brings him back to C

Rosa (*to the pony, stroking his mane*) You have very good taste, Pedro.

Bopo (*to children in the audience*) Hey, kids! How some of you like to come an' say 'allo to Pedro? Come up 'ere!

The house lights go up, and some children come up on to the stage. Bopo and Rosa introduce them to Pedro. Comic business with the pony nudging the children. Rosa asks them their names and ages. Pedro taps out their ages with his hoof. Bopo gets sweets from the wings and hands them out to the children. They return to their seats and the house lights go down. Bopo and Rosa clear to

R

To suitable music, Pedro performs a comic little dance, bows to the audience, and trots out to L

A commotion is heard UR, *and Vasaleno enters, dragging and struggling with Jack Horner. The gypsies follow and fill the back*

Meg enters DR

Vasaleno (*pulling Jack down* C) Ha. Ha! Ho! Ho! I find 'im! I find Jack 'Orner! Now I get ze reward! Ho! Ho!
Jack Let me go!
Vasaleno Hey, you must be some thief! Wot you steal, huh?
Jack Nothing! I'm not a thief! Let go of me!
Vasaleno Ha! You no go no place! You stay with me 'til I get reward! Two 'undred gold pieces! Now I take you to Prince an' collect my monies!

He drags Jack to exit DR, *but finds Rosa blocking his path*

Rosa Let him go!
Vasaleno Ah! *You* again! Outa my way!
Rosa (*standing firm*) Jack speaks the truth. He is not a criminal! Go and look in the mirror if you want to see a real criminal!
Vasaleno (*pulling out his dagger with his free hand*) Outa my way or I cuta you into leetle pieces!
Rosa Ha! You couldn't cut your way out of a paper bag!
Meg My child! Be careful!
Rosa (*to her*) I'm not scared of that inflated bull frog! (*To Vasaleno*) Let him go or—(*she whips out her dagger*) I'll let daylight into you!

Vasaleno retreats, then holds his dagger to Jack's throat. All react

Vasaleno Get outa my way or I cut your leetle friend's gizzard out! Ha! Ha! Ha!

Rosa, beaten and helpless, lowers her dagger

Bopo (*aside to Rosa*) Pedro ze pony 'elp you! Remember! (*He calls loudly*) Vasaleno!!
Rosa Of course! (*She calls*) Vasaleno! (*To audience*) You help! (*She calls*) Vasaleno!

Rosa, Bopo and the audience shout "Vasaleno!"

To suitable "charge" music, Pedro gallops on from UL. *He sees Vasaleno, paws the ground and charges at him*

Vasaleno yells in terror and releases Jack. Pedro chases Vasaleno around the stage and out UL

All cheer. Jack and Rosa move to C

Meg Rosa, you and I must leave here at once. Vasaleno will never forgive you for making him look a fool in front of his tribe.
Bopo (*to Rosa*) Meg right. 'E do you the nasties! You go *now*.
Rosa Well, Jack, it seems I *will* be running away with you after all.

Jack (*taking her hand*) Yes, and I'll do my best to look after you.

Song 13

The song ends with Rosa, Jack and Meg waving farewell to the gypsies and going out UR, *as* . . .

The Lights fade to Black-out

SCENE 2

A pathway in the woods

Tabs, or a frontcloth showing trees and bushes. Dim sinister lighting

Graball enters from down L *in a green spot*

Graball (*to the audience*) Ha! Ha! Ha! Now that everyone thinks Jack Horner is the thief I am free to carry out my second plan to steal the pearl! Unfortunately, I have a problem . . .

The audience rudely suggest he has several!

I shall need the assistance of others. I hear Vasaleno, the gypsy, is camped in these woods. He'll suit my purpose admirably! (*He looks off* R) Someone approaches! (*He clears to* L)

Vasaleno limps on from DR, *rubbing his painful bottom. Bopo follows, sniggering at the other's discomfort. Vasaleno turns in his agony and displays two large hoof prints on the seat of his pants*

Bopo (*to the audience*) Pedro ze pony do a good job, huh? (*He sniggers*)
Graball (*moving to* C) Good-afternoon!
Bopo Don't look now, but (*TV personality/politician*) is 'ere!
Graball Can you tell me where I can find Vasaleno, the gypsy?
Vasaleno (*forgetting his pain and strutting to Graball in his old boastful manner*) I am 'e. I am Vasaleno, king of all ze gypsies!
Graball I have a job for you!

He looks furtively about to make sure they are alone. Vasaleno does the same. Bopo joins in and all three get into a hopeless tangle

I want you to carry out a little highway robbery for me.
Vasaleno (*gloating and rubbing his hands*) Ho! Ho! You picka ze right man!
Graball Listen. The Royal Family have a vast fortune. Gold, jewels, diamonds and all manner of priceless objects. All of it is kept in the antiquated strong room of the Palace. The King and Queen are both fools and I can easily persuade them that the treasure would be much safer in the town's new bank vaults. I will suggest that the transfer be made at twelve o'clock tonight, under cover of darkness and with only a small detachment of guards. I will lead them through these woods and stop at

the old ruins. You and your band will be lying in wait there, and on a signal from me, you rob the wretched Royals of their entire fortune! What do you say?

Vasaleno (*rubbing his hands and chuckling with evil glee*) Hee! Hee! I like ze sound of it! It make'a my mouth water . . . (*Suddenly suspicious*) Hey! Wot *you* get outa zis, huh?

Graball There is only one thing I want. A small casket. You can keep all the rest, but you must give me the casket.

Vasaleno (*still very suspicious*) Wot's in zis casket, huh?

Graball (*quick aside to the audience*) He mustn't find out about the pearl or he'll want it for himself! (*To Vasaleno*) It belonged to . . . to my poor, white-haired old mother! (*He pretends to be very upset and fights back tears*)

Vasaleno (*his lip starting to tremble*) You . . . you 'ad a momma?

Graball (*choked up*) Yes.

Vasaleno So did I! (*He bursts into tears*)

Graball Her . . . her last words to me were—"Fluffy . . ."

Vasaleno reacts

That was her pet name for me. "Fluffy," she said, "all I own in the world is that little casket. Promise me you'll get it back." I made her a promise. That casket is all I have to remember her by!

Vasaleno goes to Bopo and cries on his shoulder. Comic business with Bopo soothing him and making a wry face at the audience. Graball comes forward

(*To the audience*) Ha! Ha! I certainly fooled that numbskull. My mother is alive and well and running her own gambling casino in (*nearby town/ village*).

Vasaleno (*coming down and putting his arm around Graball*) My friend! (*He hugs Graball*) I, Vasaleno, king of all ze gypsies, will 'elp you get back your momma's casket! (*Then back to evil normality*) An' all ze rest I get to keep, huh?

Graball Yes. It's all yours! Remember—midnight at the old ruins!

Vasaleno *I* be there! (*Villainous laugh*) Hee! Hee! Hee! (*Melodramatically, he goes to down R exit*)

Bopo (*to Graball, copying Vasaleno*) *I* be there too! (*Comic villainous laugh*) Hee! Hee! Ho! Ho! Ho!

Vasaleno grabs Bopo and drags him out DR

Graball (*to the audience*) I wonder if I've done the right thing, involving those two dunderheads? Still, no matter, once I get the pearl I shall have no further use for them. Now I must return to the Palace and set my plan in motion. Ha! Ha! At midnight I shall be the richest man in the world. Ha! Ha! Ha!

Amid boos and hisses he exits DL

A slight pause and Jack, Rosa and Meg enter from DR

Jack Did you hear that! He's still trying to steal the pearl! I've *got* to stop him!

Rosa Oh, Jack! Why bother? *Let* him steal the wretched thing! It'll prove you're not a thief.

Jack But the Royal Family will lose the pearl and the rest of their fortune. The whole Kingdom will be reduced to poverty and everyone will suffer.

Rosa So what. Why should *you* worry about any of *them*! Look at the way they've treated you.

Jack Rosa, I might as well be a thief if I stand by and let the robbery take place. I must go to the Palace and tell them what Graball and Vasaleno have planned. If I give myself up I'm sure they'll listen to me.

Rosa And if they don't?

Jack That's a risk I'll have to take.

Rosa You're a fool, Jack Horner—but, a brave one! (*She takes his hand*) You shan't take the risk alone. *I'm* coming with you!

Meg (*going to her, much alarmed*) Rosa! No . . .

Rosa Come with us, Meg. You heard them planning the robbery. Come with us and speak to the King.

Meg (*backing away*) No! . . . I . . . I can't! . . . No!

Rosa Very well. Jack and I will go alone.

She and Jack move to exit DL

Meg (*moving to* C, *and calling after Rosa*) My child! . . . Don't go! . . . I beg you! . . . *Don't go!* . . .

But they have gone. Meg covers her face in despair and exits DR *as . . .*

The Lights fade to Black-out

SCENE 3

The classroom

The same setting as Act I, Scene 5, minus the cookery table, oven and pie table. On stage, L *a blackboard and easel with rubber, chalks, etc. Three school forms are set* C, *facing the blackboard*

The children are discovered standing at the forms. Patience is at the blackboard, conducting them in a singing lesson. Bertie and Gertie wearing tall dunce caps, stand in the corner DR. *Patience sings the verse and gets the children to sing the chorus. Bertie and Gertie join in with awful, off-key caterwauling and comic contortions*

Song 14

After the song, the children sit on the forms and Patience cleans the blackboard

Bertie (*to the audience*) Coo! What a load of soppy rubbish that was! Hey kids! I bet you'd rather 'ear some real music, eh?

Gertie Yeah. Somethin' by (*latest pop group*)!

Unaccompanied, Bertie and Gertie bellow out the latest pop song and cavort about

> *Unseen by them, Dame Dimwit, in another crazy costume, enters* DL. *She stands watching their antics then moves behind them*

Eventually they become aware of her and turn the song into a sweet, angelic rendering of "Nymphs and Shepherds", ending with saintly poses

> (*Putting her hand up*) Miss! Miss! Please, miss, the school toilets are covered with filthy cracks!

Dame (*concerned*) Filthy cracks! I'll send for a plasterer at once!

Gertie No, don't! I 'aven't finished readin' 'em all yet!

She and Bertie hoot with laughter. Enraged, Dame Dimwit grabs Gertie, bends her over and raises her cane

> *The King and Peter enter from* R

Bertie sees them and immediately takes advantage of the situation by falling to his knees and clasping his hands dramatically

Bertie Mercy! Please don't do it! She's only a little girl! Have mercy!

King (*shocked*) Dame Dimwit!

Dame reacts

> What is the meaning of this? I hope you're not ill-treating the dear children!

Dame (*flustered and trying to conceal her cane*) Er ... I ... Oh, no, Your Kinglyness! (*She puts her arms around Bertie and Gertie and hugs them murderously tight*) Oh, how could anyone ill-treat these two little darlings. My favourites! Why, I love them as my own!

King (*turning to Peter*) She's just like a mother to them.

While his back is turned, Dame Dimwit knocks Bertie and Gertie's heads together and pushes them DL. *When the King turns back to her, she gives him a sweet smile*

Patience (*coming down*) Peter, is there any news of Jack Horner?

Peter He's still at large. But it's only a matter of time before he's caught.

Patience Oh, dear.

Peter Does that upset you?

Patience Well, I know he has his faults but I find it hard to believe he's a thief.

Dame Ha! I'd believe anything of that young hooligan!

Patience (*to Dame*) Shall I take the children for their next lesson?

Dame Yes, what is it?

Patience History.

The children groan loudly

Dame Ah, my favourite subject! (*To King*) I have a marvellous memory for historical events, you know.

Bertie (*moving over*) She was *at* most of 'em!

He laughs. Unseen, Dame Dimwit stamps on his toe and he hops away in agony

Peter (*to Patience*) I'd love to sit in on your class.
King (*alarmed and confused*) Do what on her where?
Patience (*smiling*) It won't be much fun, listening to me give a dull history lesson.
Peter Oh, I shan't listen to a single word—but the teacher will have my full attention. (*He takes her hand*) Come, let us make history—together!

Hand in hand, and gazing into each other's eyes, they drift to exit DR

Dame (*coughing loudly*) Ah hem! Don't forget the children!
Patience (*in a dream*) Walk this way, children.

She and Peter drift out. The children do comic, exaggerated copies of them and exit in pairs DR

Bertie and Gertie, doing the same, move to exit

Dame Just a minute, you two! Where do you think you're going?
Bertie
Gertie } (*soppy copy of Peter*) We're going to make history—together!
Dame Oh, no, you're not! You're staying here with me. I'm going to give you a general knowledge test!

They groan

King (*taking Dame aside*) Aren't those two a little old to be still at school?
Dame I know. I kept them in for something years ago and I can't remember what it was!
King May I stay and see your prowess?
Dame Oh! You rude old ruler, you!
King As a teacher, I mean.
Dame Of course! (*To the audience*) If I can remember any of it! (*She claps her hands*) Class—be seated! (*She goes to the blackboard*)

Comic business as the King and Bertie and Gertie fight to sit on the same form—King getting pushed off the end, etc. Finally, Dame Dimwit sorts them out and they each sit on a separate form

(*At the board*) Now then, get yer brain boxes in gear! (*To the audience*) And pay attention at the back, because I'll be asking *you* questions later. (*To the three*) Question one.

The following are only suggestions. Other gags can be used or a different routine, if desired

What kind of bear would you find at the South Pole?
Bertie (*hand up*) A *lost* one!
Dame Stupid boy! Name three types of bear!
Gertie (*hand up*) Daddy bear, Mummy bear and Baby bear!

Dame (*to the audience*) I walked right into that one, didn't I? (*To the three*) Who can name one deadly poison?—and don't say the school dinners!

Bertie (*hand up*) I can miss!—Tightrope walkin'!

Dame That's not a deadly poison!

Bertie Oh, yes it is! One *drop* an' you've 'ad it!

Dame I'll drop *you* in a minute! Now a geography question. Where are the Andes?

Gertie (*hands up*) On the end of your armies!

The three hoot with laughter. Dame bangs her cane on the blackboard

Dame Order! Order! I must have order!

Bertie Mine's a cheeseburger an' chips!

Laughter. Dame bangs her cane

Dame Silence in class! Now, what is a—

King (*hand up*) Miss! Miss!

Dame (*sweetly*) I've started so I'll finish. What is a slug?

Gertie (*hand up*) A slug is a snail with a housing problem!

King (*hand up*) Miss! Miss! Ask *me* a question.

Dame Very well, Your Kingship. A maths question for you. If you had a five pound note and you asked Mrs Queen for another one, how much would you have?

King Five pounds!

Dame (*wagging her finger at him*) Ah, you don't know your maths.

King (*glumly*) And you don't know my old woman!

Dame Who was Noah's wife?

Gertie (*hand up*) Joan of Arc!

Dame Bertie, how would you spell the word—"correctly"?

Bertie *In*correctly, I expect miss!

Laughter. Dame bangs her cane

Dame Right, smarty-pants, answer this one! If you had five sweets and I took away one, how many would you have left?

Bertie Four—an' *you'd* 'ave a black eye!

Dame What is a comet?

King (*hand up*) I know, Miss! It's a star with a tail on!

Dame (*gushing*) Very good sire! Can you name one?

King Yes! Champion the Wonder Horse! (*or Lassie!*)

Laughter. Dame bangs her cane

Dame Can anyone give me a sentence with the word "mayonnaise" in it?

Bertie }
Gertie } (*waving their hands*) We can! We can!

They stand up and sing "Mayonnaise have seen the glory of the coming of the Lord"

Dame Sit down! Here's one for you, Your Maj. Please give me a sentence—

King Twenty years!

Laughter

Dame (*with a forced laugh*) How droll! (*To the audience*) Silly old twit! (*To the King*) Give me a sentence with the word "fascinate" in it.

King (*standing up*) Er ... Oh, yes! My shirt has got ten buttons, but I can only—"fascinate"! (*He bows and sits*)

Dame Gertie, come out to the blackboard and spell the word "needle".

Gertie goes to the board and chalks on it. She spells it—NEIDLE

Silly girl. There's no "i" in needle!

Gertie It's not much good then, is it?

Dame takes a swing at her, but Gertie ducks and scuttles back to her seat

Dame Now we'll go on to the really hard questions. What is—

Bertie (*hand up*) Miss! Miss! You said you were goin' to ask *them* some questions! (*He points to the audience*)

Dame So I did! (*To the audience*) Now it's your turn, my little Magnus Mackesons. Here's a question for you. What do you think of it so far?

Audience Rubbish!

Dame Correct! Give yourselves ten out of ten!

The Queen sweeps on from DR, *followed by Graball*

Queen Marmaduke!

King (*reacting*) Hell ... (*he turns to the Queen, all smiles*) ... Lo, my dear. Lovely to see you ...

Queen (*brushing him aside and taking* C *stage*) Jack Horner, the thief, has been captured! (*Calling off* R) Bring in the prisoners!

The guards enter DR, *escorting Jack and Rosa, and take them before the King and Queen. Peter, Patience and the children and some of the townsfolk enter upstage*

Jack Your Majesty. I've given myself up to speak to you—

Queen Be silent! We do not wish to hear anything from a common thief!

Rosa But you *must* listen to him!

Queen *Or* from a common gypsy!

Peter (*coming down*) Mother, it would do no harm to hear him. After all, he did give himself up. (*To Jack*) What have you to say?

Jack In the first place, I did not steal the pearl. He did. (*He points at Graball*)

General reaction. Graball soon covers his guilt with outraged indignation

Graball This is preposterous! (*To the King*) Sire, I appeal to you! Must I endure this outrageous accusation!

Peter On what grounds do you accuse the Lord Chamberlain?

Jack I *saw* him do it with my own eyes!

Dame Jack Horner, you're at it again! More fibs! You can't believe a word that boy says!

Rosa But, it's—

Queen Silence! This boy is obviously a liar as well as being a thief! To the dungeons with him!

Rosa But, there's more to tell! We both overheard a plan to— ·

Queen Enough, gypsy! Since you choose to share his life of crime, you will have no objection to sharing his dungeon cell! (*To guards*) Away with them!

Protesting, Jack and Rosa are taken out by the guards DR

Queen Marmaduke! You have taken up enough of Dame Dimwit's time. I'm sure she has lessons to attend to—*now*!

Dame Oh, yes! Come along, Miss Patience, get the children ready for their next lesson ... er ... what ever it is ...

Bertie You said you was goin' to take us for a nature ramble in the woods!

Dame So I did! Ah, there's nothing like a nice nature ramble! Oh, I *love* nature!

Bertie That's nice of you—considerin' what nature did to *you*!

He and Gertie snigger

Dame Get out!!

She pushes them out DL, *and follows, giving the King a soppy wave. Peter, Patience, the children and the Townsfolk exit upstage*

Queen Marmaduke—home!

King Yes, dear.

Graball Your Majesties, I am very concerned about the safety of the pearl.

Queen Why, Lord Chamberlain? It's quite safe. it's locked away in the Palace strong room with all my other valuables.

King Her spare set of choppers. Her Lady Grecian 2000. Her plastic surgeon's phone number. Her——

The Queen slaps him

Graball You may not be aware, Your Majesty, that the strong room is rather antiquated. It would be easy prey to robbers, and now with something as priceless as the pearl ...

Queen (*very alarmed*) Oh! I see what you mean! (*Grabbing the King in a panic*) Marmaduke! What shall we do?! (*To Graball*) What do you suggest we do?

King (*to Graball*) Yes, go on, be suggestive!

Graball The bank here in town has a marvellous up-to-date vault. I would suggest that the pearl and the rest of the royal treasure be transferred there, without delay.

Queen Of course! (*To the King*) Well, don't just stand there! See to it! (*She pushes the King to exit* DR)

Graball Wait, sire! Is it wise to carry out the transfer in broad daylight? Why not do it tonight—say at midnight, under cover of darkness. (*Very oily*) Allow me to attend to the whole matter, Your Majesty. (*He bows*)

Queen Thank you, Lord Chamberlain. I know I can trust *you* to do it properly. (*Glaring at the King*) Unlike *some* people who haven't got the brains they were born with! (*She sweeps to exit* DR)

The King sticks out his tongue at her departing back

I saw that! Wait till I get you home!

She exits

The King does a double-take, then follows her, rather puzzled

The stage darkens. Green spot on Graball

Graball (*to the audience, gloatingly*) Ha! Ha! Ha! The first part of my plan has worked! Soon the pearl will be mine! *All mine!* Ha! Ha! Ha!

Amid boos and hisses, he exits DR

The Lights return to normal. Music

Peter and Patience enter DL, *going straight into a song. If desired, the townsfolk and children can enter and join them in the song and dance*

Song 15

After the song, the Lights fade to Black-out

Scene 4

The pathway in the woods

Tabs, or the frontcloth used in Act II, Scene 2. Dim eerie lighting. A roll of thunder and a flash of lightning

Dame (*off* L) Yoo hoo! . . . Anyone there? . . . Cooee! . . . Children, where are you? . . . Oh!

Thunder and lightning. Dame Dimwit creeps on backwards from DL *She is scared, weary and very lost. She is comically dressed for a nature ramble with huge, baggy shorts, enormous Girl Guide's hat, shirt smothered with badges, etc. On her back is a rucksack with all manner of objects hanging from it, a plastic potty, sink plunger, toilet roll, etc.*

(*Looking about her, forlornly*) Oh, no! I'm back in the same place again! I brought the children into these woods this afternoon for a nature ramble. I just nipped behind a tree to . . . er . . . admire the peas and leeks . . . and when I came out, they'd all done a bunk! The little creeps! That was hours ago, and I've been wanderin' about in these wild woods ever since!—Lost! I've missed (*TV show for that day*) because of them! Oh, those perishin' pupils! I'll brain 'em for leaving me in this fix!

Eerie "ghostly" moaning (Bertie and Gertie) is heard off R. *Dame reacts*

(*Gulping*) W-w-what was that? (*To the audience*) Did you hear it?

The moaning is repeated

Oo! There it is again! . . . Oh, they say these woods are haunted!

The moaning is repeated, louder

I-i-it's getting nearer . . . it's g-g-ghosts! (*She cowers down* IC, *with her hands over her eyes and her knees knocking*)

Bertie and Gertie creep on from DR. *They wear comic Scout and Guide uniforms. They tiptoe to each side of Dame Dimwit and make ghostly noises*

(*Shuddering with fear*) Ooo! . . . G-go away, ghosties! . . . W-what do you want? I'll do anything, just go away! . . . Ooo!

Bertie (*in a deep, eerie voice*) We will go away on one condition!
Dame W-what's that?
Bertie (*as before*) You must repeat these words—I am a silly old twit!
Dame I am a silly old twit!

Bertie and Gertie have silent hysterics

Bertie (*ghost voice*) I have a face like a stewed prune!
Dame I have a face like a stewed prune!

Bertie and Gertie move away R, *and giggle uncontrollably. Dame Dimwit opens one eye, then the other. She sees them and reacts, then tiptoes over behind them*

Bertie Coo! This is great! We can get old droopy drawers to say anythin' we like, she's that scared! Come on, let's 'ave some more fun with 'er!
Gertie Yeah. Bags it's my turn!

They creep back with Dame creeping up behind them. They are startled to see the empty space

Bertie Hey, look!
Gertie She's gone!
Bertie Crikey! She's vanished!
Gertie (*shaking*) Oh, Bertie, I'm scared! Per'aps there really are ghosts an' they carried 'er off!
Bertie Ha! It'd take more than ghosts to carry 'er off! You'd need a fork-lift truck! (*To the audience*) Hey kids! Did you see what 'appened to old Dimwit. Where is she?
Audience Behind you!

Comic business with Bertie and Gertie turning around and Dame Dimwit keeping behind them. "Oh, no, she isn't"—"Oh, yes she is!" routine. Eventually, they come face to face with her, yell and try to make a getaway

Dame (*grabbing them*) Oh, no you don't! So. You want to be ghosts eh? Well, I'll soon arrange that!
Bertie Please, miss! We didn't mean no 'arm. It was just high spirits. Ha! Ha! . . . Get it? Spirits . . . ghosts! Ha! Ha . . . (*His laughter dissolves into a cough as he sees the Dame's grim expression*)

Bertie and Gertie start wailing loudly, and pretending to be "frightened little children", rush to Dame and cling to her

Gertie Me fwightened!
Bertie Me fwightened too!
Dame (*dismayed*) Frightened? I haven't started on you yet!
Bertie We're lost in the woods!
Gertie I wanna go 'ome!

They wail and bury their faces into Dame, pulling at her shorts. Comic business. Dame Dimwit forgets her anger and is completely taken in by their act. She puts comforting arms around them

Dame (*cooing*) There, there. Don't crysy wisey. Nice Dame Dimwit's here. She'll take care of you. Didums. (*She hugs them tightly*)

Unseen by her, Bertie and Gertie grin and give each other the "thumbs up" sign

I'll soon have you out of the nasty old wood and tucked up in your own little bedsy wedsys. (*She takes them by the hand*) Let's go home. If we go this way ... (*She leads them* DR, *then stops*) No, we'll go *this* way ... (*She leads them* DL, *then stops*) No, we'll go *this* way ... (*She leads them back* DR, *then stops and dithers*)

Bertie ⎱ (*sing-song*) You're lost!
Gertie ⎰
Dame (*bringing them* C) Lost! Me? Never! (*She shows a badge*) Look! I've got my tenderfoot!
Bertie With feet that size, I'm not surprised!
Dame If only we could find someone to ask. There's never a policeman about when you want one!
Bertie (*looking off* R) Hey! Here's two men!
Dame Men?! Oh! (*She preens herself*)

Vasaleno strides on from DR, *followed by Bopo. Both wear black cloaks and black masks ready for the robbery*

Oh, look! We're in luck! It's Ratman and Bobbin! (*To Vasaleno*) Hallo, Caped Crusader!
Vasaleno (*growling at her*) Wot for you doin' 'ere?
Dame (*to the audience*) Doesn't he talk funny? Must be from (*neighbouring town or village*). (*To Vasaleno*) I wonder if you can help me. I'm in a quandary.
Vasaleno No, you ain't! You in a *wood*! Ha! Ha! (*Grisly laugh*)
Dame (*to the audience*) Scarcy so-and-so! (*To Vasaleno*) I've lost my whereabouts.
Vasaleno Well, I ain't got 'em on! You no business 'ere. (*Flamboyantly*) All zis wood my private properties! I am Vasaleno, king of all ze gypsies! You get away from 'ere. Scat!
Dame (*to the audience*) Oh, what a rude romany! (*To him*) How dare you speak to me like that! I'll have you know I'm very big in this area!
Vasaleno Ha! You very big in *all* areas! Ha! Ha! Ha!

Bertie and Gertie laugh. Dame glares at them

(*To Dame*) Leeson to me, baggy bloomers ...
Dame (*outraged*) Well, really!

Vasaleno If you ain't gone by ze time I count to three … (*He pulls out his dagger*) I cut you into leetle pieces!

Dame Dimwit yells and hides behind Bertie and Gertie

An' zat goes for Bill an' Ben too!

Bertie }
Gertie } (*wailing, genuinely, this time*) I wanna go 'ome!!

Vasaleno (*advancing a step*) One!
Dame (*as all three back away*) But, we're lost!
Vasaleno (*another step*) Two!

The three just shiver and shake in terror

Three!! (*He leaps at them*)

Dame, Bertie and Gertie scream, jump in the air, and run out DL

Vasaleno roars with laughter. Bopo joins in, rather weakly

(*To the audience*) They bigger cowards, zan you!

Audience reaction

(*To Bopo*) Soon it be midnight, then we nick ze royal treasure! (*Melodramatically*) To ze old ruins!

With a swirl of his cloak he exits DL

Thunder and lightning

Bopo (*a bad copy*) To ze old ruins!

He tries to swirl his cloak, but gets in a mess with it and blunders out DL

Thunder and lightning, then the Lights fade to Black-out

SCENE 5

The haunted ruins at midnight

A spooky, sinister looking place. At midstage C, *there stands the crumbling remains of a tower with a high practical archway. Fallen masonry is dotted about the stage and some form a jagged ground row at the back. The wings represent tumbledown, overgrown walls and twisted trees. The backcloth shows a dark, storm filled sky*

Dim, eerie lighting. Ground mist, if possible. Sinister music. A roll of thunder and a flash of lightning

The gypsies, armed with daggers and clubs, creep on from all directions and go into a wild song and dance

Song 16

After the song, there is thunder and lightning

Vasaleno enters and strides to C, *laughing his villainous laugh. Bopo follows, looking very scared*

Vasaleno Ha! Ha! Ha! My loyal band!
Gypsies (*gathering around him*) Hail, Vasaleno!
Vasaleno 'Tis midnight! Time for us to do ze dirty 'ighway robbery! (*Villainous laugh*) Ha! Ha! Ha!

The gypsies laugh villainously. Bopo is shaking with fear

(*To him*) Hey! Wota matter for you?! Why *you* no—Ha! Ha! Ha!—like ze rest?!
Bopo (*gulping*) T-too scared!

Vasaleno and the others roar with laughter

Vasaleno Zis robbery be piece o' cake for ze mighty Vasaleno an' 'is tribe! No need for you to be ze cowardy custard!
Bopo I ... I no scared of ze robbery ... I scared of ... zis *place*! (*In hushed tones*) Zis place ... it '*aunted*!

Thunder and lightning. All, except for Vasaleno, jump with fright and cling to each other in terror

Zay say it 'aunted by ze 'orrible, 'ideous ghost. An' all who see ze 'orrible, 'ideous ghost, die ze 'orrible, 'ideous death!!

Thunder and lightning. The gypsies tremble and start to creep away. Vasaleno stops them with a bellow

Vasaleno Hey!! Where for you go?!
Gypsy W-we no want to see g-ghost!
Gypsy W-we no want to die ze 'orrible, 'ideous death!
Vasaleno (*with a scornful laugh*) Ha! There are no such thing as ghosts! I, Vasaleno, king of ze gypsies, no believe in ghosts! They just pigments of ze imagination! You stay!—or *I* give you ze 'orrible, 'ideous death!

The gypsies dither uncertainly

Bopo Ze ghost walk at midnight!
Vasaleno I no care if it ride ze skateboard! (*He grabs Bopo by the ear. To the gypsies*) 'E just make up zis scary stuff to frighten you out of doing ze robbery! That wot you do, huh? (*He twists Bopo's ear*).
Bopo (*in agony*) Ahh! ... Yes! Yes! ... I make it up! ... I make it up! ...
Vasaleno (*to the others, throwing Bopo from him*) See! Wot I tell you!

He and the gypsies laugh and jeer at Bopo. A gypsy, who is on look-out, sees something off L

Look-out Vasaleno—they come!
Vasaleno (*calling them to order*) My tribe! To ze 'idin' places! Wait for ze signal! *Go!*

The gypsies conceal themselves behind the ruins

(*To the audience*) Soon Vasaleno will be ze richest man in ze world! Ha! Ha! Ha!

He goes to exit, bumps into Bopo and drags him out DR

Thunder and lightning

A slight pause. Graball enters from L, *leading the King, Peter and four guards. The King carries the pearl casket and the guards are carrying two treasure chests*

Peter Lord Chamberlain!

All halt

Are you sure this is a short cut to town? We'd have been better off staying on the main path. You seem to have taken us miles out of our way.

King Yes. All this flippin' walkin'! (*Holding up a painful foot*) I've got bunions on me bunions, and this box is starting to weigh a ton!

Graball Rest assured, sire, you will soon be relieved of it . . . in the bank vault.

King Well, don't let's hang about in *this* place! (*He looks about, nervously*) They say it's haunted by a horrible, hideous ghost! Let's get moving! The Queen is waiting up for me, and she needs her beauty sleep! (*To the audience*) Oh, *how* she needs it! (*To Graball*) Let's get on with it!

Graball (*with a mocking bow*) Certainly, sire! . . . (*He suddenly moves* R, *and calls loudly*) Now!!

Thunder and lightning. Dramatic music as Vasaleno and the gypsies spring from hiding and surround the startled group

Vasaleno (*roaring*) Take ze treasure!!

After a brief struggle, the gypsies overpower Peter and the others and hold them captive. The chests are brought to Vasaleno, who opens one and gloats over its sparkling contents. Graball gives a mocking laugh

King (*utterly confused*) Lord Chamberlain! . . . What is the meaning of this?

Graball snatches the casket from the King and hugs it lovingly

Graball At last! Mine! All mine!

King I say! You can't do that! Peter, he's pinched our pearl!

Peter Yes! Jack Horner was speaking the truth all along! You blackguard . . . !

He tries to pull free, but the gypsies hold him fast

Vasaleno (*going to Graball*) My friend, wot we do with zem, huh? Shall we . . . ? (*He makes grisly, throat-slitting gestures*)

Graball There's no need to get our clothes messy. We'll put them in there— (*he points to the tower*)—and seal up the entrance! They'll die from starvation! By the time their bones are discovered, we shall be thousands of miles way, living in luxury!

Vasaleno Ho! Ho! I always wanted to live there! (*To gypsies*) Put 'em inside!

The gypsies push Peter and the others towards the tower. Suddenly, loud ghoulish laughter echoes from the tower. (An off-stage microphone should be used for this.) Everyone freezes. The laughter is repeated

Bopo Ze ghost! It's ze ghost!!

Thunder and lightning. Sinister music. The stage grows dark and eerie (UV lighting if possible). All back away from the tower

A tall, white shape appears in the tower archway. It glides DS and hovers. This "apparition" is Gertie sitting on Bertie's shoulders. Both are completely covered in a long, flowing white sheet. The ghost raises its shrouded arms. Thunder and lightning. The ghoulish laughter is repeated

Another ghost (Dame Dimwit in a white sheet) appears DR

Bopo and the gypsies scream with fright and run out in all directions

The tall ghost staggers and sways, then collapses in a heap C. The lighting returns to normal. Bertie and Gertie crawl out from under the sheet

Graball It's a trick! Run for it!

He and Vasaleno run to exit DR, but get entangled with Dame Dimwit

Peter Men! Seize those two villains!

The guards rush across, grab Vasaleno and Graball and hold them captive. Dame Dimwit, engulfed in her sheet, falls to the ground and continues to struggle with thin air

Dame Have at you! ... Take that! ... Zap! ... Kerpow! ... Biff! ...

Bertie and Gertie go to Dame and pull the sheet off her. She is revealed with her bottom sticking up towards the King

King I recognize that face! It's Dame Dimwit!
Dame (*standing and giving a salute*) Never fear, Dimwit's 'ere!
Peter (*taking the casket from Graball*) I'll take that! (*He gives it to the King. To a guard*) Run to the Palace! Inform the Queen of what has happened and have Jack Horner released immediately.

The guard runs out L

King (*confused*) Dame Dimwit, I don't understand ...
Dame It's simple. We were lost in the woods, and sheltered in that old ruin because of the storm. Then old face-ache and his gypsies came along. We overheard everything! All about the robbery and—the ghost! The gypsies were scared stiff and that gave me a brain wave. *We'd* pretend to be ghosts and frighten 'em off. And, by jolly hockey sticks, it worked!
Bertie (*to her, artfully*) Aren't you goin' to explain where we got the white sheets from in the middle of a wood? (*He winks at the audience*)
Dame (*clamping her hand over his mouth*) Sher up! It's called artistic licence.
King Well, you certainly saved the royal bacon! (*To Graball*) And as for *you*! (*Confronting him, boldly*) I've got one thing to say to you!

Graball (*pulling forward and snarling*) What?!

King (*recoiling*) Er ... You've been very, very naughty. So there! That poor lad, Jack Horner! How we all misjudged him.

Dame Well, I always thought he was telling the truth.

They all look at her, reproachfully

Queen (*off* L) Marmaduke!

She sweeps on from L, *followed by Jack, Rosa, the guard, Patience, the children and some of the townsfolk*

(*Going straight to the King*) I can't leave you alone for five minutes! I understand there has been another attempt to steal my pearl!

King Yes, my dear, but everything is all right now. Look.

He shows the casket and she snatches it away

The real thief has been arrested. It was the Lord Chamberlain all the time!

Queen (*giving Graball a withering look*) I'm not surprised! (*To the King*) This is all *your* fault!

King (*to the audience*) I had a feeling it might be!

Queen You should have gotten rid of that man years ago. I always said he was shifty! (*To the guards*) Remove those persons from the Royal sight! To the—

King Please let me dear! (*To the guards, very much the King*) To the dungeons with them!

Amid boos and hisses, Graball and Vasaleno are lead out DL. *Graball shakes his fist at the crowd, and at the audience as he goes*

Jack Horner, please accept my Royal apology for not believing you.

Jack (*bowing*) Thank you, Your Majesty.

King (*to the Queen*) Well, my dear, aren't you going to say sorry?

He greatly enjoys putting her on the spot. The Queen sticks her nose haughtily in the air. Everyone leans forward, looking at her with eager anticipation. At last she gives in

Queen (*an inaudible mumble*) I'm sorry.

King (*revelling in her discomfort*) What was that, my dear? I didn't quite catch it. (*Hand to ear*)

Queen (*roaring at him*) I'm sorry! Sorry!!!

The King staggers back, deafened

Meg enters DR

Meg Rosa!

Rosa (*rushing to her*) Meg!

Queen (*glad to be "top dog" again*) Arrest that old woman! She's one of the gypsies!

Meg I am *not* a gypsy! (*Moving to the Royals*) Your Majesties ... Prince Peter ... Don't you recognize me?

Peter Wait a minute! ... Surely it's ... yes! It *is*! It's our old nurse maid!
Nursie! (*He hugs Meg*)

General reaction

King Great sufferin' sceptres! Peter's right, my dear! It *is* old nursie! (*He
hugs Meg*) Nursie!

Queen (*pulling him away and confronting Meg*) Nurse! What is the meaning
of this?! We thought you were dead! How dare you suddenly come back
to life again after all this time! Fifteen years ago you left the Palace in
charge of our orphaned niece, the Lady Caroline. You never returned!
Nurse, what became of that child?

King (*to Meg*) We searched for months ... (*sadly*) She is dead?

Meg No, sire. She is alive! *There* she stands (*She points to Rosa*) There is
Lady Caroline!

General uproar and amazement. Rosa is the most amazed of all

King (*going to Rosa*) Why, yes! ... I can see it now! Oh, Caroline! ... Come
to nunkie! (*He hugs the bewildered Rosa*)

Rosa But ... What's all this about? ... I'm Rosa, the gypsy ... I'm not
Lady Caroline ...

Meg You *are*, my dear! I've kept it from you all these years.

Queen Nurse! I demand an explanation!

Meg That morning, fifteen years ago, I took little Caroline for a walk in
these very woods. We got hopelessly lost and wandered into a gypsy
camp. I was too frightened and confused to tell them who we were. They
suggested that we travel with them. I knew I was in terrible trouble for
failing in my duties as a nurse maid and feared your anger. So, I agreed to
go with them. Over the years Caroline, or Rosa as she became known,
looked upon the gypsy folk as her real family. She was so happy and
contented, I didn't have the heart to tell her of her true identity. We
travelled the World and only last week returned to your Kingdom. (*She
kneels before the King*) Your Majesty, can you ever find it in your heart to
forgive a foolish old woman.

King Rise, dear old nurse.

Meg does so

I forgive you, and thank you for remaining with our niece all these years
and keeping her safe from harm.

Rosa rushes to Meg and hugs her

(*To all*) Oh, joyous day! The pearl is safe! The villains are under lock and
key, and our dear niece returned to us! Loyal subjects, you all have my
royal permission to let you hair down, and—go bananas! Whoopee!!

All cheer, General rejoicing

Queen (*bellowing over the din*) Marmaduke!

All go silent

King (*to the audience*) I thought it was too good to last! (*To the Queen glumly*) Yes, dear?
Queen (*sternly*) Come here!

He goes to her, expecting the worst

(*After a slight pause*) Whoopeee!! (*She hugs the King tightly and plants a noisy kiss on his cheek*)

All cheer

King (*thrilled, amazed, jubilant*) Oh, Maggie!! What can I say???
Jack Your Majesty, there is only one thing left to say ... (*He comes forward with Rosa and sings*)

Song 17

A joyful song for everyone. Bertie and Gertie get into mischief and are chased out by Dame Dimwit. After the song, a frontcloth is lowered or the tabs close

SCENE 6

The last lesson

Frontcloth or tabs

Dame Dimwit skips on to C, swinging a long cane. She wears a comic hat and gown easily changed for the Finale walkdown

Dame (*waving to the audience*) Hallo, my little scholars! You've been a marvellous audience. The best we've had all night. You've been so good I'm giving you all top marks for attendance and A plus for laughing in all the right places. (*Pointing to someone*) Even *that* naughty little boy/girl who kept fidgeting all the time! Now there's just one more lesson before school's out. A singing lesson! Ah, you thought you'd got away with it, didn't you! (*She calls off*) Bertie! Gertie!

Bertie enters R, and Gertie enters L. Both carry song-sheet boards with the blank side showing to the audience

Here they are! My star pupils! They make Einstein look like Worzel Gummidge! (*To them*) Have you got the lyrics?
Bertie No, we always stand like this!
Dame Stupid boy! Have you got the words?
Gertie Yeah!

They hold up their song sheets

Dame Oh, I see! Don't tell me, we're all going to sing *Silent Night*! Turn 'em round!

They do so. Each have the words to two different songs

Oh, no! That's no good! You've both got different words! Oh you stupid ... students, you!

Bertie *That* lot—(*he points to his side of the audience*)—can sing *this* song ...

Gertie An' *that* lot—(*she points to her side of the audience*)—can sing *this* song!

Bertie }
Gertie } (*together*) At the same time!!

Dame (*to the audience*) And may the best man win! Now, I want to hear you all singing, or I'll keep you all in! (*To conductor or pianist*) Belt it out, Beethoven!

Song 18

They have fun getting the audience to sing the two songs at the same time. Comic business and ad lib. After the song, they run out, waving and calling "Bye! Ta! Ta!" to the audience

SCENE 7

The grand finale

A special setting or the Palace scene from Act I can be used. Fanfare

Music, and all enter singing for the Finale walkdown. The last to enter are Jack and Rosa

Jack The time has come to say Farewell, our pantomime has ended.

Rosa Everything has turned out swell, as always was intended.

Graball You speak for yourself! We're off to the nick!

Vasaleno Oh, shuta your face! You maka me sick!

King The wifey kissed me, and I want some more! (*He cuddles the Queen*)

Queen Marmaduke, please! Not in front of the poor!

Peter (*to Patience*) Let's be married, and the knot we'll tie.

Patience Then I'll be a Princess, just like Lady Di!

Dame Oh, how Barbara Cartland!—But where's my Romeo?!

Bopo I no Jason Donovan, but I try to 'ave ze go! (*He hugs Dame*)

Gertie All you kids must be alert, while sitting in your class ...

Bertie An' if you're not, you'll get the cane, right across your...

All No!!

Jack If you've come from miles away, or just around the corner.

All We hope you've had a smashing time—good-night from Little Jack Horner!

Final Chorus Song 19

CURTAIN

FURNITURE AND PROPERTY LIST

ACT I

SCENE 1

On stage: Town backcloth
Playground wings with comic graffiti
Low wall with school gates
School with "Dimwit's School" sign

Off stage: Slates, satchels **(Children)**
Brightly painted pram. *On it:* motor horn, L-plates, stickers, aerials, flags, etc. **(Bertie and Gertie)**
Large fake lollipop **(Bertie)**
School bell, cane **(Dame)**
Cane **(Dame)**
Casket containing large black pearl **(Graball)**
Broken cane **(Dame)**

Personal: **Graball:** pouch on belt with fake pearl
Dame: pince-nez (required throughout)

SCENE 2

On stage: Tabs or frontcloth

Personal: **Bertie:** blindfold in pocket, bag of sweets in pocket

SCENE 3

On stage: Palace backcloth
Palace wings
Stairs and archway
Cut-out pillars and chandeliers
Dais. *On it:* large throne marked "Hers", smaller throne marked "His"
Wall tapestries painted on flats

Off stage: Casket containing fake pearl **(Guard)**

Personal: **Graball:** pouch on belt with real pearl

SCENE 4

On stage: Tabs or frontcloth

Off stage: Basket. *In it:* heather, pegs, charms, ribbons **(Rosa)**
Basket. *In it:* heather, pegs, etc. **(Meg)**
Bag of jelly babies **(King)**

SCENE 5

On stage: Classroom backcloth
Classroom wings
Large table. *On it:* check cloth, mixing bowls, flour shaker, rolling pin, "crazy foam", dough, etc. *Under table*: 2 perfect uncooked pies
Smaller table. *On it:* check cloth
Trick, exploding oven with practical door
Stage cloth

Off stage: Pies, to be passed through back of oven for children **(Stage Management)**
2 burnt, "smoking" pies for Bertie and Gertie **(Stage Management)**
"Crazy foam" to be sprayed from oven **(Stage Management)**

Personal: **Gertie:** comic items for search
Bertie: comic items for search
Graball: pouch containing pearl

ACT II

SCENE 1

On stage: Wood backcloth
Wood wings
Large cut-out caravan with practical door and steps
Smaller cut-out caravans
Camp fire with cooking pot
Barrels and boxes

Off stage: Sweets for children in audience **(Bopo)**

Personal: **Gypsy dancers:** tambourines
Vasaleno: huge fake chicken leg, dagger
Rosa: small dagger

SCENE 2

On stage: Tabs or frontcloth

Personal: **Graball:** handkerchief
Vasaleno: 2 stick-on hoof prints, big, spotted handkerchief

SCENE 3

On stage: Classroom backcloth
Classroom wings
Blackboard on easel. *On it:* chalk, blackboard rubber, canes
3 wooden school forms

Off stage: Cane **(Dame)**

Personal: **Bertie** and **Gertie:** tall "D" caps

SCENE 4

On stage: Tabs or frontcloth

Personal: **Dame:** badges, rucksack with plastic potty, sink plunger, toilet rolls etc.
Vasaleno: black cloak, black mask, dagger
Bopo: black cloak, black mask

SCENE 5

On stage: Night sky backcloth
Ruined tower with practical archway
Ruin ground row
Ruin and tree wings
Bits of fallen masonry, etc.

Off stage: Daggers, clubs, masks **(Gypsies)**
Casket containing pearl **(King)**
2 treasure chests containing coins, jewels, etc. **(Guards)**
Long, white "ghost" gown **(Bertie** and **Gertie)**
"Ghost" gown **(Dame)**

SCENE 6

On stage: Tabs or frontcloth

Off stage: Long cane **(Dame)**
Song sheet boards **(Bertie** and **Gertie)**

SCENE 7

On stage: Special Finale setting or as Act I, Scene 3

LIGHTING PLOT

Property fittings required: chandeliers for I, 3; camp fire effect for II, 1

Various interior and exterior settings

ACT I, SCENE 1

To open: General exterior lighting

Cue 1	**Jack** sings *Fade to special "dream" lighting*	(Page 6)
Cue 2	"Dream" characters exit *Stage darkens. Spot on* **Jack**	(Page 6)
Cue 3	**Dame:** "Jack Horner!!" *Cut spot. Return to previous lighting*	(Page 6)
Cue 4	**Graball** sneaks to centre stage *Lighting dims slightly. Green spot on* **Graball**	(Page 10)
Cue 5	**Peter** enters *Cut spot. Return to previous lighting*	(Page 11)
Cue 6	**Peter** sings *Fade to "romantic" lighting*	(Page 12)
Cue 7	After **Song 5** *Return to previous lighting*	(Page 12)
Cue 8	**Bertie, Gertie** and children charge out of school, yelling and shouting *Fade to black-out*	(Page 13)

ACT 1, SCENE 2

To open: General exterior lighting

Cue 9	**Bertie:** "I've got to go down there!" *House lights up*	(Page 16)
Cue 10	**Bertie** returns to stage *House lights down*	(Page 17)
Cue 11	**Gertie** chases **Bertie** out *Fade to black-out*	(Page 18)

ACT I, SCENE 3

To open: General interior lighting; chandeliers on

Cue 12	**King** takes **Dame** upstage *Lighting dims slightly. Green spot on* **Graball**	(Page 20)

Cue 13	**Graball** laughs. **Dame** and **King** turn	(Page 20)
	Cut spot. Return to previous lighting	
Cue 14	**King** goes to sleep on throne	(Page 23)
	Fade to black-out	

ACT I, SCENE 4

To open: General exterior lighting

Cue 15	**Guards** exit	(Page 24)
	Lighting dims. Green spot on **Graball**	
Cue 16	**Graball:** "... knowing you! Ha! Ha! Ha!"	(Page 24)
	Cut spot. Return to previous lighting	
Cue 17	**King** exits	(Page 27)
	Fade to black-out	

ACT I, SCENE 5

To open: General interior lighting

No cues

ACT II, SCENE 1

To open: General exterior lighting; camp fire effect on

Cue 18	**Bopo:** (*to the audience*): "Come up 'ere!"	(Page 35)
	House lights up	
Cue 19	Children return to their seats	(Page 35)
	House lights down	
Cue 20	**Jack, Rosa** and **Meg** exit	(Page 37)
	Fade to black-out	

ACT II, SCENE 2

To open: Dim, sinister exterior lighting

Cue 21	**Graball** enters	(Page 37)
	Green spot on **Graball**	
Cue 22	**Graball:** "Someone approaches!"	(Page 37)
	Cut spot	
Cue 23	**Meg** exits	(Page 39)
	Fade to black-out	

ACT II, SCENE 3

To open: General interior lighting

| Cue 24 | **King** exits | (Page 45) |
| | *Lighting dims. Green spot on* **Graball** | |

Cue 25	**Graball** exits	(Page 45)
	Cut spot. Return to previous lighting	
Cue 26	After **Song 15**	(Page 45)
	Fade to black-out	

ACT II, SCENE 4

To open: Dim, eerie exterior lighting. Flash of lightning

Cue 27	**Dame:** ... "Children, where are you? ... Oh!"	(Page 45)
	Flash of lightning	
Cue 28	**Vasaleno:** "To ze old ruins!" He exits	(Page 48)
	Flash of lightning	
Cue 29	**Bopo** exits	(Page 48)
	Flash of lightning, then fade to black-out	

ACT II, SCENE 5

To open: Dim, sinister lighting, then flash of lightning

Cue 30	After **Song 16**	(Page 48)
	Flash of lightning	
Cue 31	**Bopo:** "Zis place ... it 'aunted!"	(Page 49)
	Flash of lightning	
Cue 32	**Bopo:** "... die ze 'orrible, 'ideous death!!"	(Page 49)
	Flash of lightning	
Cue 33	**Vasaleno** drags **Bopo** out	(Page 50)
	Flash of lightning	
Cue 34	**Graball:** "Now!!"	(Page 50)
	Flash of lightning	
Cue 35	**Bopo:** "Ze ghost. It's ze ghost!!"	(Page 51)
	Flash of lightning, special lighting (UV if possible) for "ghost"	
	(Bertie *and* **Gertie)** *entrance*	
Cue 36	"Ghost" **(Gertie)** raises its arms	(Page 51)
	Flash of lightning	
Cue 37	"Ghost" **Bertie** and **Gertie)** collapses to ground	(Page 51)
	Return to previous lighting	

ACT II, SCENE 6

To open: General lighting

Cue 38	**Dame, Bertie** and **Gertie** run out	(Page 55)
	Fade to black-out	

ACT II, SCENE 7

To open: Bright, general lighting

No cues

EFFECTS PLOT

ACT I

Cue 1	**Before CURTAIN rises** *School bell rings*	(Page 1)
Cue 2	**After Song 2** *School bell rings*	(Page 3)
Cue 3	**Jack starts to sing** *Ground mist*	(Page 6)
Cue 4	**Herald enters through gates** *Fanfare*	(Page 6)
Cue 5	**Herald: "... Prince Peter!"** *Fanfare*	(Page 7)
Cue 6	**After Song 5** *Whacking and wailing from school*	(Page 12)
Cue 7	**Jack exits** *School bell rings*	(Page 13)
Cue 8	**Queen slaps King's face** *Loud "slapstick" or cymbal crash*	(Page 14)
Cue 9	**Graball: "Miss Patience!"** *Fanfare*	(Page 19)
Cue 10	**Graball: "... BA and public bar!"** *Fanfare*	(Page 19)
Cue 11	**King and Dame look into oven** *Flash and loud bang as oven explodes, flashes and smoke; "crazy* *foam" sprayed over **King** and **Dame** from inside oven*	(Page 30)

ACT II

Cue 12	**To open SCENE 4** *Roll of thunder*	(Page 35)
Cue 13	**Dame: "Children, where are you? ... Oh!"** *Roll of thunder*	(Page 45)
Cue 14	**Vasaleno: "To ze old ruins!" He exits** *Roll of thunder*	(Page 48)
Cue 15	**Bopo: exits** *Roll of thunder*	(Page 48)

Cue 16   To open SCENE 5   (Page 48)
           Roll of thunder, ground mist

Cue 17   After **Song 16**   (Page 48)
           Roll of thunder

Cue 18   **Bopo:** "Zis place ... it 'aunted!"   (Page 49)
           Roll of thunder

Cue 19   **Bopo:** "... die ze 'orrible, 'ideous death!"   (Page 49)
           Roll of thunder

Cue 20   **Vasaleno** drags **Bopo** out DR   (Page 50)
           Roll of thunder

Cue 21   **Graball:** "Now!!"   (Page 50)
           Roll of thunder

Cue 22   **Vasaleno:** "Put 'em inside!"   (Page 51)
           *Loud, ghoulish laughter (on off-stage microphone) comes from
               tower, pause then repeat laughter*

Cue 23   **Bopo:** "Ze ghost! It's ze ghost!"   (Page 51)
           Roll of thunder

Cue 24   "Ghost" **(Bertie** and **Gertie)** raises its arms   (Page 51)
           Roll of thunder and repeat ghoulish laughter

Cue 25   As SCENE 7 opens   (Page 55)
           Fanfare

MADE AND PRINTED IN GREAT BRITAIN BY
LATIMER TREND & COMPANY LTD PLYMOUTH

MADE IN ENGLAND

MADE AND PRINTED IN GREAT BRITAIN BY
HAZELL WATSON & VINEY LTD, AYLESBURY, BUCKS
MADE IN ENGLAND